I SEE COLOR

IDENTIFYING, UNDERSTANDING
AND REDUCING OUR HIDDEN
RACISM: A WHITE PERSPECTIVE

Robert L. Pellegrino

To my daughter, Alicia. May her generation and the generations that follow, find an America that affirms their humanity and beauty, in keeping with its promise.

Table of Contents

Acknowledgments

Acknowledging and reducing my racism has been a lifelong process which is always ongoing. As such, nearly everyone I am close to, or have dealings with, contributed to this process in different ways.

I am grateful to my Mom and Dad, and my siblings—Karen, Lynn, Lisa and my late brother, Louie—for allowing me the freedom to discuss racial issues with them, even though I know they find it uncomfortable. They've come a long way in understanding the complex issues surrounding race relations in this country.

The same holds true for my lifelong white friends: Bobby, David, Cappy, John, Billy, Lummy, Gerry, Frank, Mike, Bruce, Sam, JJ, and Skip. I know all of them care deeply about me and they accept me for who I am and what I believe in. They, like my family, love and respect my wife and daughter as they would anyone else.

20 years ago a group of like-minded white people came together for the first meeting of our Speak Out Against Racism group (SOAR). I learned a lot from them. One thing I learned was how difficult it is for white people to specifically deal with our racism. Bobby Foreman, an original member of that group, was one of the few white people who ever taught me about my racism. Another original member, Margaret Conable, once told me that this book would get finished at the appropriate time, so I shouldn't stress about it. Her words have echoed through my mind time and again, as I've struggled with work and family obligations while working on this book.

My first black friend, Jeff, who I met at Bowdoin College, got me started on this journey, planting the seeds to what would become my "knowledge-through-experience" revelation about race relations.

Donald Day, former captain in the Bridgeport Fire Department and past president of the Firebirds society, is one of my earliest black friends (nearly 35 years). Throughout my life he has mentored and supported me in this process.

There are a few people without whom this book would never have been written. First and foremost is my editor, Peter Heyrman. He tirelessly assisted me in the organization and coordination of my jumbled thoughts, articles, and analysis into a manuscript that would eventually become this book. He then stayed on me to finalize it for publication. I'm convinced that you would not be holding this book in your hand if not for Pete. He made my dream a reality.

Tim Parrish is a phenomenal writer, professor and best friend. He not only helped me hone my rudimentary writing skills, but, as a rare white man, he dialogued with me for hours on the issue of white racism, probing, sharing and discussing many thoughts on the subject.

I have been truly blessed to have Michael Jefferson who has been both a best friend and mentor for nearly 30 years. I may never know why he has taken the time and effort and patience to educate me on such a personal and difficult subject as race. His friendship has opened the doors to so many enlightening experiences that it's impossible to recount them all here. But his family –especially his wife, Pam, and his friends (Gary, Kermit, Larry, Greg, Steve and others) have allowed me into their homes, and their discussions, and they have trusted me enough not to edit those discussions in my presence.

It is impossible to recount the many ways in which my wife, Danielle, and my daughter, Alicia, have taught me about race and racism in both direct and indirect ways. While dealing with

Acknowledgments

racism in their daily lives, they allowed me the space to stumble and flounder on more complicated issues, while patiently and subtly guiding and directing me to a deeper understanding of racism. I now know the complex responsibility of protecting and supporting them in this society, and I am humbled by the love and trust that they show me each day.

Foreword *by Michael A. Jefferson*

"I found him! I think I found him!" yelled my former college roommate. He beamed as he approached me on Orange Street in downtown New Haven. It was 1988 and the presidential election was just months away. The two of us, along with a couple of dozen other young activists, had just completed a successful voter registration drive. It was one of those hot, late summer days, and my friend had left the group in a desperate search for water. He'd found relief on the fourth floor of the one of the office buildings on the narrow block—in the law office of Robert Pellegrino.

Earlier I'd told my friend that I needed to find Pellegrino. At the time all I knew about Bob was that he'd written a brief letter to the New Haven Register in response to an article they'd run a few weeks earlier. Forty Greater New Haven "leaders" had been asked to respond to the question: "What is the most pressing problem facing the region?" In my article I cited "racism." No other respondent had raised this issue.

Pellegrino's letter praised my article, while expressing disappointment that only one individual had seen this as the most pressing problem. His words conveyed his annoyance and bewilderment. When I read his response I too was taken aback, but for different reasons. I had never encountered a white person who openly displayed such anti-racist sentiments. I was shocked. So I set out to find Robert Pellegrino from North Branford. It was a daunting task. One wonders how we ever found anyone without social media.

When my friend told me he'd found Robert Pellegrino, I was

elated but cautious. I'd known plenty of whites who "talked the talk" but didn't "walk the walk." I had experienced far too many disappointments from whites who claimed to be "progressives." As my friend led me to 209 Orange Street, the building that housed Pellegrino's law office (and later my own), I could not stop thinking: "I hope this dude doesn't disappoint me."

I'd heard the old argument that racism was really just a part of a "class" struggle, but too often this was just whites making excuses for the racism of other whites. I was fed up with whites stopping Blacks from defining our oppression, though white women and white ethnic groups were perfectly free to define theirs. "When will whites just shut the f*#k up, and listen to us?" I would ask my black friends. These thoughts raced through my mind as I went to meet Robert Pellegrino.

Our initial encounter went well. On his office wall was the iconic photo of the brief Capitol Hill encounter between Malcolm X and Dr. King in 1964. Seeing that displayed so conspicuously helped put me at ease. I was accustomed to whites embracing Dr. King and his legacy, but it was surprising, to say the least, to see a white man paying homage to Malcolm X. I savored the moment, but knew, as soon as the opportunity presented itself, I would revisit the matter.

We later met for lunch, and, from his questions, it appeared Bob was as eager to pick my brain as I was to pick his. We talked about Malcolm X, Louis Farrakhan, the separation of the races and a lot more. Years later he told me he wasn't quite ready for that initial conversation. I was surprised by that admission only because he never gave any hint of unease, by word or gesture. For me, it had the first time I'd been able to fully articulate my feelings as a black man to a white man, directly, without being interrupted by "opinions" on race or racism. This made Bob unique. It has been a huge part of the foundation of our friendship and brotherhood ever since.

Over the years I have come to see Bob not only as one of

my very best friends, but also as a unique social scientist. I owe much of what I understand about the white psyche pertaining to race, to him. I recall asking him: "Why is it that whites seem to tune out black folks in meetings and round table discussions?" His response was simple: "Mike J, most white people don't think a black person can teach them anything." "It's that deep, Bob P?" I asked. He simply looked at me, his expression leaving no doubt about the answer.

Our many discussions on race have led me to examine more deeply the inferiority complex of black people. I surmised that if whites are socialized to harbor a false sense of superiority about themselves, then Blacks living within the same society, and undergoing a similar socialization process, must be socialized to develop a false sense of inferiority about ourselves. This revelation made it easier for me to completely abandon ownership of the fight against racism. As far as I was concerned, Blacks have our own challenge: confronting our false sense of inferiority.

Rather than spending so much time fighting racism, Blacks must turn the mirror on ourselves, so we can question the inferiority complex that continues to wreak havoc on the black psyche. By understanding this challenge to the black community, I came to a deeper understanding of the challenge confronting the white community about racism. "Bob has a tough road ahead." I thought to myself back then. I'm sure he knew it, but he seemed eager to accept whatever might come.

Bob would often tell me how he challenged family and friends to confront their own individual racism, as well as society's. "Some get it, Mike J, but most don't want to get it," he would say. "Think about it like this: How many whites have Blacks over for dinner? How many whites watch black movies or read books about Blacks? How many whites try to understand the black experience?" I never knew the answers, but I certainly got the gist. Bob is not only thought-provoking, he's honest.

Much of what you will encounter in this book comes from his willingness to listen to the black voice uninterrupted. He is also brutally honest in his assessment of the white psyche. When dealing with race and racism, Bob takes no prisoners.

When I first met his future wife—Danielle, I was struck by her noticeable connection to the black community and culture. It was unusual for me to meet a black woman who could date a white man, and still be so wedded to her roots. I found this fascinating. I have come to see that most whites erroneously assume that all blacks have a similar bond to the broader black community. In reality, there are many Blacks who shun the black community while seeking acceptance from the dominant culture. I guess some Blacks feel that the racial reality invites them to go to great lengths to escape it. In our first conversation I learned Danielle was not having any of that "nonsense." As the reader will see, Danielle had an immediate impact on Bob's developing racial perspective.

When he was in the company of my friends, most of whom were black and distrusting of whites, Bob often challenged me to "keep it real." Bob did not want or expect any special consideration when hanging out with the "fellas." While at times he was spared, many times he was not. While watching sporting events with my crew, Bob would hear the dialogue of the "black" fan in the privacy of his own dwelling, or in a place where he felt comfortable expressing himself.

Unbeknownst to most whites, many black sports fans understand the underlying racial dynamics of white commentaries on athletes. We know what it means when a player is described as having a "blue collar" work ethic. We know whom the commentators are referring to when they describe an NFL player as a "possession" receiver, or a college basketball player as a "heady" player. We know what they mean when they refer to a player as a "talented athlete." We know there is a huge preference for white quarterbacks in the NFL, and that they are given every opportunity to succeed. We watch as black players are condemned for fighting in the NBA, yet white players are given the green light in the NHL because "it's part of the game." In many instances our racial sensitivities carry over to the commercials, and we dissect them from a racial perspective.

Some of this dialogue was, no doubt, awkward for Bob, but I tend to think most of it was quite enlightening. Bob was willing to go through this racial "baptism," and listen to the black perspective on American sports. This was a unique experience for him, as well as my crew and me. Most Blacks I know rarely speak honestly about race in the company of whites. Many Blacks consider it a complete waste of time. The chance of having such moments might seem even more remote when watching a seemingly innocuous "game." But, as Bob discovered, the twin issues of race and racism are an inescapable feature of the black existence.

Bob and I both attended predominantly white Catholic high schools, and we participated in athletics at our respective schools. Aside from that our experiences were vastly different. Much of what Bob later learned about the experiences of a black student attending a predominantly white school, he got from talking with black friends he met in college, and later, others, like me, who were similarly situated. He would also learn from the experience of his daughter—Alicia.

Bob would often describe the racism endured by his daughter at the predominantly white school she attended. He found white school administrators to be surprisingly unsympathetic and cavalier in addressing this issue. They seemed unaware of the racism that awaited Alicia at school each day. It wasn't news for me.

Like most parents, my mom simply wanted her children to receive the best education they could get. I took a test to enter a celebrated, predominantly white high school in the Bronx. I was accepted. While I met good people, and enjoyed success as a high school athlete, if I had to do it over, I would not. Unlike the previous public schools I'd attended, the classroom atmosphere at my high school was uninviting. I never found the work particularly challenging. I simply found the support from teachers and their level of expectation to be wanting. My involvement in sports probably made it easier to navigate the predominantly white social terrain, but nonetheless I felt like an outsider. My high school experience was tolerable only because I found reasonably effective defense strategies and coping mechanisms.

So when Bob shared some of Alicia's experiences I wasn't surprised at all. What was disheartening was the degree of racism still prevalent in the next generation. Clearly, racial progress was fleeting. Anyone suggesting otherwise was delusional. I couldn't help but think of the millions of black students all across this country, at every grade level, who have shared similar experiences. I remember a high school reunion dinner where a former white classmate came up to me and said: "Back in our day we didn't have as many problems with racism as we do today—huh, Mike?" I gave him a blank stare then looked away. I was speechless.

"I See Color" is a must-read for whites who truly want to wake up to the truth about race and racism in American society. The book provides an intelligent analysis of the problem, real life experiences of black family members and friends, painfully honest depictions of racism within the author's own family, and thought-provoking solutions for combating America's ancient sin.

Whites who are honest about challenging racism, and are willing to unlearn their racism, while enhancing their understanding of its causes and effects, should read this book and encourage others to do the same. In writing this long overdue book Bob Pellegrino has done a great service to our society. His determination to save the souls of those belonging to the dominant culture is both timely and commendable. The work begins now.

Introduction

I write this book with trepidation. I know of nothing that causes so much hostility, misunderstanding and hurt feelings among whites than the issue of race. I write for whites. Black people already know the problem. Whites are the ones who struggle to understand it, always fearing that our efforts will unearth the roots of our own self-indictment.

In his autobiography, Malcolm X wrote of being approached by a young white woman who asked what she could do to help his cause. He turned her away brusquely, saying there was nothing she could do. Later he reflected that he wished he had told her to go into her own community—the white community—to educate them about their racism. His words moved me to go back to my own community where I could work with other white people to overcome our racism.

A half century after the Civil Rights laws of the '60s whites still avoid real discussions about race and racism, and how it applies to each of us, and our communities. We've found plenty of euphemisms over the years, buzzwords that let us imagine we're addressing the problem, while all we're really doing is putting egalitarian window-dressing on patronizing concepts and programs. We advocate "diversity" and "multi-culturalism," but ignore the stark specter of racism that still looms over all of us. We use these buzzwords to avoid the more difficult path: discussing, defining, and understanding our legacy of racism so that we might overcome it in ourselves.

It is the duty of whites to end racism. It's an uncomfortable responsibility because it stems from guilt. It's a disturbing obligation because its roots are in a history we can't change. We didn't sail to Africa, we didn't capture people, we didn't chain them up, ship them over here, or buy them when they reached these shores. We didn't lynch anyone, blow up any churches, or bar young black children at the schoolhouse door—but our people did. Generations of white people built and supported a system that guaranteed white advantage. That system's main support was belief in our own superiority. In doing so, whites created a legacy of hate, misunderstanding, and an attitude of black inferiority that lives on to this day. That is the racism you and I live with. It's the racism we are passing to our children. It's real, palpable, and when we practice it (which we do without even knowing it), African Americans feel it. And we diminish ourselves in the process.

Whether conscious or unconscious, our racism has real repercussions. It is the reason black-owned property is worth less than white-owned property. It's why historically black colleges and universities are considered the poor relations in our higher education system. In areas of health, transportation, communication, and virtually all public services, whites get a better deal than Blacks. These are the effects of our racism. Blacks deal with it every day. Many whites don't even know it's there.

After nearly 30 years of work in race relations, I am not so naïve as to believe my fellow whites will simply "jump on the bandwagon" and try to root out their racism. Rather, most whites will never pick up this book. Most of you who do will either fail to finish it, or dismiss most of what I have to say. However if even a few of you accept my premise that whites must actively acknowledge and examine our racism, and if you can move from that to the idea that we must help each other do this through reflection, discussion, education, and good will, then the book will be worth it.

I don't intend this to be a "scholarly" piece. I haven't

included copious footnotes, statistical quotes, graphs or charts. I want this book to be readable and engaging, much like a good conversation. You may agree or disagree, but make no mistake: what follows is not simply another white man's opinion. This work springs from the knowledge and experience that come from decades of living with, working with, and caring about black people and white people. I have dealt with racism in broad areas of policy, and in the most personal ways. If white people are going to effectively counter the barrage of daily misinformation about black people here and in the Diaspora, we need to educate ourselves from their scholars. So I've studied history from Diop, Clarke and Van Sertima, psychology from Akbar, Kunjufu and Cress-Welsing, social studies from Madhubuti, Karenga and Asante, feminism from Hooks and Giddings, and from others who are experts in this field.

Let's be clear: opinion is not knowledge. Understanding our racism and how it manifests itself is obtained through studying the works of others and from experience. Much in the same way that learning history, sociology or psychology is done.

Few white Americans have spent the majority of their adult lives analyzing and researching the issue of racism. I have. I've spent thousands of hours in conversations with Blacks and whites about race. I've read book after book about the African experience in American history, and their earlier history in Africa. I've also read widely, receiving a personal education in European history, race relations, and mental health issues that touch on race. I've pored over many "solution-based" books on America's racial problems. I established a non-profit organization designed to deal with white racism, and co-produced a local TV show here in Connecticut where Blacks and whites discussed issues of race. Almost everything I have learned about whites and racism has been from black people—authors, directors, teachers, friends and family.

I have had the wonderful, enlightening and sometimes

painful experience of interracial marriage. My wife, Danielle, and I have an African American daughter, Alicia, and I've been lucky enough to have black friends, especially a close one— Mike Jefferson—who challenge me daily with their insights and perspectives. That's what understanding racism is for whites—a monumental challenge. You can't simply erase racism with information or knowledge. You must also attack it using self-examination and an open mind. You must be as open and honest as you can possibly be.

Recognizing, understanding and reducing racism is a process, and for whites it is never complete. It evolves. Often I thought I'd progressed enough to feel certain of one answer, only to see later that it wasn't complete, or even correct. I learn by paying attention. Listening to my wife, daughter, and friends is my continuing education. I hear many of the same things you hear, but instead of getting my information from a news report, or a magazine article, it's there in my home. Often my reflexive reaction to stories of racism are the same as yours: I resist belief. But whenever I force myself to look at these stories objectively I find they are true. The racism is there. Usually it finds that the best hiding place is out in plain sight. We don't see it because it fits seamlessly into our world. We accept it because we don't see it.

If there's anything I want this book to be, it is a call to whites to open our ears and listen, and open our eyes and look. We must try to set aside our opinions, and listen to what Blacks really say. When we hear something uncomfortable, we must resist the urge to walk away. Instead, we should listen and look even more carefully.

If you don't have close friends who are black, read black authors, go to movies produced, directed and/or acted by Blacks, listen to black music and go to black plays. Pick a subject that interests you, then view it from a black perspective. At the end of this book you will find lists of suggestions. Whenever you experience a situation where race plays a role, try to look at it through black eyes, and listen carefully for the nuances of race, both black and white. Whenever you find yourself trying to be "color-blind," or eliminating race from your thinking, do the opposite: look at the situation in terms of race, and its effects.

For those of you who start down this road please note that it will strain almost every white relationship you have, whether it be with friends, relatives or members of your immediate family. Nothing raises white defenses as quickly or surely as the mention of race. I won't go into all the theories about why this is true. Each may have some foundation in truth, but our defensiveness is a high hurdle to jump. If knowledge of racism's causes helps us root it out, fine, but many of those causes long predate us. These include environmental, biological, and psychological issues, among others. Whites began our racist journey with the first voyage of a slave ship. White attitudes about violence and our own superiority predate even that. The main thing we need to do now is to recognize the racism in ourselves, accept its grim legacy as our responsibility, and start the long process of recovery. That will be different with every individual, but the issues will be the same. We must work to understand our own racism so that we can do all we can to eliminate it—or at least know it for what is really is. If you are willing to take the risk, the reward is a giant step toward the truth. That's always liberating.

Throughout the eras of slavery and Jim Crow many whites, including philanthropists like Cecil Rhodes, and religious institutions like the Mormon Church, contended that black people had no souls. It was a part of their justification for their crimes. My journey has led me to the opposite side of the question. Often I've found myself asking whether we white people have souls. We are the ones who left our homes behind to sail to foreign shores and subjugate others. We are the ones who invaded their lands, attacked their customs, and robbed them of freedom. We murdered, tortured and dehumanized Blacks. We would like to think we've changed, and indeed most of us have, but our inhumanity lives on in thousands of subtle ways. I write this book to further the cause of rediscovering our humanity so that we might become who we hope to be.

Chapter One

◆

Unlocking Our Minds

*I tell sincere white people, 'Work in conjunction with us—
each of us working among our own kind.' Let sincere white
individuals find all other white people they can who feel as
they do—and let them form their own all-white groups, to
work trying to convert other white people who are thinking
and acting so racist. Let sincere whites go and teach non-
violence to white people!*

*We will completely respect our white co-workers. They will
deserve every credit. We will give them every credit. We will
meanwhile be working among our own kind, in our own black
communities—showing and teaching black men in ways
that only other black men can—that the black man has got
to help himself. Working separately, the sincere white people
and sincere black people actually will be working together.*

*In our mutual sincerity we might be able to show a road to
the salvation of America's very soul.*

—Malcolm X

We are at our best when we want to learn more, and at
our worst when we act out of ignorance. If you are a
white American like me, this book is about overcoming our
ignorance, and learning as much as we can about our racism
and about black Americans. It's not an easy goal…

What if I told you that growing up in America predisposes
you to harboring racist sentiment towards African Americans?
Would you dismiss it out of hand? If so, could you accept a

different idea: that American men are predisposed to sexism? If so, how do they get this predisposition? There's only one possible source: their upbringing. American men learn to be sexist from music, film, sports, school, music, church, home, relationships and the magazine rack at the corner drugstore. White Americans learn racism the same way. We can readily admit that sexism still exists, and point to evidence of that, so why can't we get whites to accept our racism?

Accepting the possibility that any accurate picture of American life will include racism is the same as accepting that we all might have racism within us simply by growing up in America. If you can accept that as a possibility and "wear it" for awhile like a new shoe, you might liberate yourself from the denial which prevents any real learning from taking place. Once I admitted my racism to myself —conscious and unconscious— I felt a huge burden lift, freeing me to fight my own racism. The first, and most difficult goal of all, is to open our minds to this reality

As you begin you may find it impossible to decipher all the reinforcing mechanisms of racism, but if you learn to look at our world with an African American perspective you will see them clearly. Racism runs like an undercurrent through our media, workplaces, political campaigns, schools and every other part of society.

A lot of this racism is visible to even the most casual observer, but there are many invisible effects as well. Whether it is explicit or implicit, racism is alive, well, and affects us every day. There are four general categories of our racism. First, there is the obvious racist, such as the skinhead or white supremacist. Second, there is the conservative who believes we all have an equal chance in life, and we need to "get over" the racial talk and move on. The third is most of you reading this book: You believe in equality, and know that the failure to achieve it is due to the continued existence of racism. You want to help out in some way. Finally there are some white people who understand the depth and impact of racism, examine themselves and their actions deeply, and try to counter its existence. I count myself as one of them, but other more notable examples are Tim Wise, Peggy McIntosh and Andrew Hacker, to name a few.

Ask yourself this question, and answer it honestly: where did I get my information on race and race relations? And then ask yourself: is it an opinion based upon other opinions or is it based upon knowledge?

I write this book for those of you who want to reach that fourth category. I have struggled as you have. I will show some of my struggles with my own racism, and I will begin by admitting how much sexism I ignorantly harbored long into adulthood. I began a similar journey by listening to women, especially my sister, Lynn. It's been a long, difficult road for me, but I have begun to grasp some of sexism's complexity. If some of you do the same with racism, your efforts will move this giant boulder a few feet forward. If that happens it will be your doing. I can describe how racism works, and show its effects, but in the end only you can convince you.

Think about it: in school we learned white history, white culture, and white heritage. We, the white people, sailed the ocean, fought the battles, cleared the fields, built the roads, and made the decisions. We invented everything from the light bulb to the silicon chip. We wrote it all down in the history books. And what about African-Americans? We brought them here, we traded them like cattle, we fought a war over their status, then one of our great leaders freed them.

What do we really know? To us black history doesn't really begin until Africans are herded off the slave ships at our ports, and even then we think of them only as a group. If you doubt this, then try to name even a few famous African Americans from before the 20th century. Most of us can rattle off plenty of whites from George Washington to Jesse James to Dolly

Madison. We know about writers like Twain, Poe and Harriet Beecher Stowe, pioneers and explorers like Daniel Boone and Kit Carson, and adventurers such as Davy Crockett and Jim Bowie. Most of us know a few of the 25 presidents before 1900, and we would recognize the names of most of the others. Many of us can recall generals, like Grant, Lee, and Sherman, or a songwriter like Stephen Foster. Inventors like Thomas Edison and Alexander Graham Bell come to mind.

But famous Blacks? Some of us might come up with Nat Turner. A few might recall a name like Harriet Tubman or Frederick Douglass. But what do we know about them? Did they chop down any cherry trees? Die at the Alamo? Blaze a trail west? If not, then what did they do? Few whites know.

To many of us, real black history—the kind that tells stories of individuals—starts with Jackie Robinson, rises through Martin Luther King, and peaks with Barack Obama. To us black culture begins with jazz, or maybe even later, with soul or rap. Our knowledge of black literature might extend to the plots of a couple of books, or maybe just a couple of titles or authors—or it might be nonexistent. A few of us know who Spike Lee is, but how many of his 20-plus films can we name?

Most of us don't know anything about the Africans who preceded Columbus to this hemisphere, or the Middle Passage, or about the various lands where African Americans originated. All we know is that somehow they got here, and that was a problem from the start. We wanted slaves, and there were always some among us willing to make their living by filling that demand. We wanted obedient drones; we got human beings. Our ignorance began in our denial of that truth.

Once we disposed of the truth, it was easy to substitute the myth of our own supremacy. That myth has dominated our thinking ever since, sometimes consciously, but more often subconsciously. Indeed, if you are practicing racism consciously, then you won't be helped by anything I say. Almost all whites of good will and intention practice it unconsciously and therefore need to uncover it, and expose it. If we want to rid ourselves of this subconscious notion that we are superior, we have to educate ourselves about the people whom we regard as inferior, giving their history and culture the same chance we give our own. We must examine the arrival of the slave ships with the same scrutiny we give to those European immigrants who landed at Ellis Island. We must look at the plantation from a slave's perspective, giving their stories the time, effort, and respect that we give to the immigrant experience. More than that, we must learn the differences between the two.

For white immigrants assimilation was difficult. For enslaved Africans it was illegal, and sometimes punishable by death. For the children and grandchildren of Africans it remained unacceptable, and usually impossible. White immigrants, who came seeking freedom, could learn the ways of America, while adapting their own cultures to this new world. Enslaved Africans had been robbed of both their freedom and their culture. If on entering an American port the slave ships had sailed past a statue of liberty it would have been the cruelest joke imaginable. These Africans persevered by holding onto whatever they could in order to create a new culture. Once they had gained even a little freedom, they struggled to uncover links to their past. Whites have paid little attention to these efforts. We prefer the comfort of our own well-documented world.

So our second goal is to go back beyond the slave ships, and learn the kinds of things about African Americans that we already know about ourselves. What kinds of civilizations did they come from? How were they captured? How did they cross the ocean? What did these 1-out-of-8 Americans do before Jackie Robinson, Lena Horne or Martin Luther King came along? To begin with, we must read, watch, listen and ask questions. It's not easy. We have to want to do it. Then we have to do more. We have to acknowledge that we don't know them. And we have to seek out information on how they experienced America, right up to the present day.

Learning about our fellow Americans of African descent is a steppingstone to fighting our own racism. It helps us recognize that we are not superior, and they are not inferior. It's hard to think of someone as equal if you know nothing about them. Though we might not be able to entirely erase our own ingrained racial attitudes, we should want to learn what racism is, how it developed, why it's wrong, and what we can do to keep ourselves from passing it on to the next generation.

Only after we have taken the time to learn about African American history and culture can we begin to recognize, reduce and eliminate our own internal racist feelings. Once we begin to do this we might help other whites do the same. Once we have some grounding in the history and culture, we can pass this knowledge to the next generation. We must teach African American history and culture to our children to give them a better understanding of their fellow Americans, black and white.

Our aim in these initial efforts is to change perceptions. We must learn enough to realize that we see through white eyes, hear with white ears, and think from a white point of view. Then we have to set that viewpoint aside, and try to perceive the world through black sensibilities.

The last step in this beginning will be to change our behavior, which means changing our habits. Our most effective tool in denying our racism is habit. If we live our daily lives in an all-white world our racism seems academic. When we speak of it at all, we speak only to each other. When we look for solutions, we look to each other. We're right to examine ourselves to define the problem, but the only way to solve it is to approach African American individuals, communities and culture on their own terms, just as they've done with us for centuries. We must do this with the same courtesy, respect and care that we give to each other (and that African Americans have given us). That often means showing ourselves to be open, available and interested, while waiting for them to invite us in. If we try to impose ourselves on their community they will have the same reactions we have to unwelcome intruders: resentment and rejection. So we follow a two-pronged strategy: approaching Black America through history, literature, and culture, then applying what we learn to our habits—attending movies, lectures, workshops, plays and exhibits that reinforce and deepen our knowledge. We want to make our recovery from racism into an everyday part of our lives.

This starts with one person: you. If you are a normal white American you've probably gone through life thinking of yourself as being free of racism. Parents, teachers, clergy, and mentors all told us not to hate anyone on the basis of race, color or creed. We soaked this up in our white homes and neighborhoods. We learned it in nearly all white schools. Most of us agree that we shouldn't hate African Americans, but what about that uncomfortable feeling we get when we see a young black man on the street? What about avoiding black neighborhoods? Or black schools, or churches, or even movies or restaurants?

Your first step on this journey might be a book. It might be history, or sociology, or pop culture. It could be biography, or a novel. Or, if you're a film buff, you could start by watching a few movies. Do you like any music from African Americans? Have you listened to it all your life? Don't just listen to it; learn about it. Are you a sports fan? Start reading African American sports writers, and learn the history and heritage of black sports in America. Do you like popular history? Go to the bookstore or library, and look for African American history by African American authors. You'll be amazed by how much you'll find. If you don't know where to start, go to the back of this book.

There you'll find a list of books and movies by Blacks about black life.

Start with yourself. Look at what you do every day. Look at your neighbors, your co-workers, your children's classmates, your fellow patrons in coffee shops, drugstores and supermarkets. Are they almost all white? Who were the last ten African Americans you talked to? Were they on the other side of the counter? Or the other side of a dinner table? All the while, be open to the possibility that racism is there in almost everything you see and feel.

This isn't to say that you should go right out and befriend the first African American you meet. The first step is to begin preparing to meet African Americans as equals who have a rich, vibrant culture that covers every aspect of life. This initial effort is to orient yourself so that you can begin to see life through their eyes. That's what culture is all about: seeing life through the eyes of others.

Once you've acclimated yourself, and tasted the richness of African American life, you can start on the other goals. At that point you'll have learned something you can teach your white friends. You'll be ready to delve deeper into the African American experience. Eventually you might even find yourself connecting with black acquaintances and friends. They're already familiar with your culture. They have to be. That's why your first goal must be that of returning the favor: read, watch, listen, and learn about their world. While doing this, learn about yourself, and try to understand why you've missed out on this huge part of your world. And reach for a new level of sophistication on the issues. Open your mind, and examine your own attitudes. Keep a sharp eye out for denial.

Reduction and elimination of denial is the flip side of learning. As you steep yourself in black culture and black life, you will see details of your own racial biases at every juncture. Your first reaction will be to do what most of us do every day of our lives: deny it. Don't. Whenever you see something that makes you shake your head, stop, and examine it more closely. If a notion seems wrong or ridiculous, stop, and consider ways that it might not be either one. Look at yourself through a black person's eyes. Do you have a family tree? Do you know what ancestors came over on the boat? Were they escaping a stifling life in the old country? Were they seeking freedom? How would it be if your great-great grandfather had been caught in a net, beaten into submission, then chained into the hold of a cargo ship with hundreds of other victims? What if on landing here he'd been stripped of his name, punished for any sign of his own talent, intelligence, or culture, and sold to the highest bidder? What if he started a family with your great-great grandmother, only to find himself sold to some faraway owner? What if his children were sold off, one-by-one to work on plantations in other states you'd never heard of? It was against these odds that African Americans developed one of the most influential cultures in North America. Understanding that culture, and our long and continuing denial of it, is one of our most important goals.

We pursue these goals through our choices. Some of these decisions are big, and long term: Where do we buy our next house? What schools do we pick for our children? Other choices are more immediate: What movie do we watch? What class do we take? Where do we go on Saturday night?

A thousand small choices and a few big thoughts will lead us to our ultimate goal: to do all we can to check our own racism and that of others. A first step is that of admitting the problem.

We might begin by treating this as a meeting of a recovery group. Recovery groups know that the first step is always that of dealing with denial. We spend our lives telling ourselves and others that we aren't racists. Because I'm writing this book, I'll be first to step up to the podium and announce: "I am racist." Perhaps more accurately, I harbor racist sentiments or beliefs, most of which are subconscious.

And as you sit in your folding chair, surrounded by your fellow white newcomers, you might ask: "What's that supposed to mean?"

It means that I'm a white American; born-and-bred, with all the advantages that brings. I grew up in a nice white house in a nice white neighborhood. I went to a nice white school. I was expected to go to college and find a profession. I did so in a white world. Everything I learned, in school, at home and in life, reinforced my race, and my people, as right and dominant. My race makes my life easier every day. Most of the time I don't notice it, but when I talk to my black wife or my black best friend, I realize how much frustration I avoid just by being white. Even in 2015, more than a half century after the Civil Rights Movement began, I have a huge head start. Statistics prove that, but experience proves it better. We can't make ourselves into African Americans, with their upbringings and histories, and we should not deny our race's role, and our own part, in enslaving, denigrating, and exploiting them. To do that we would have to change the past, coming right up to the present. But we can reverse that in ourselves. We can make the effort, starting by reading, watching, and listening. If we do that we can begin to learn from them.

When that white woman approached Malcolm X, asking what she could do to help African Americans and he curtly answered: "Nothing," he later said: "I'm not proud of that answer. I should have talked to her about working in the white community... The problem exists among white people."

As a white American I'm trying to follow his advice. I'm writing this for white people who agree that racism is a problem that must be solved. I'm writing for any of you who feel that the goals I've outlined are worthwhile. We need to realize that it's NOT the racism that makes us bad people; rather, it's our continuing failure to address it head-on. That failure makes us unable to fulfill our potential as human beings. If you're willing to consider the idea that you might be racist, and you're ready to read, listen, and do the work, then this book can be your introduction to solutions. We won't solve the problem of racism, but maybe we can learn how to face it, and reduce it, so our children might bear less of a burden.

Chapter Two

♦

The Man in the Mirror

Like most white Americans my racism, and my denial, were right there in my upbringing. I was raised in a small white town in the northeast. We were Italian-Americans, as were most of our neighbors. I didn't see a black student in a classroom until I was in high school.

I wasn't completely unaware of racial problems. When I was seven my father and I witnessed the aftermath of a fight between a black man and a white man at an ice cream stand. Both men were there with women. The white man's forehead was bleeding a little, and there was shouting. The black woman seemed scared for her husband. Rage burned in the eyes of the white couple. I'd seen anger and fights before. Kids fought at school, and sometimes people got violently angry on the street. This was different. At this ice cream stand white rage inspired black fear. I don't know if race sparked the fight, but it was the fuel feeding the white couple's ugly passions.

Over a decade later, in 1975, I went to Bowdoin College, a bastion of the liberal arts in the white isolation of Brunswick, Maine. By that time I saw myself as a white liberal. I felt like I wasn't denying anything. I knew my country had a long history of racism. I also knew that there had been a Civil Rights Movement. Just a decade earlier demonstrations, marches and riots had changed laws, customs, and social mores. Blacks could sit in the front of the bus. They could go to white public schools, eat at white lunch counters, and stay in white hotels. I'd learned that these changes were good. Equality was good. Someday soon society would be color-blind. That was the goal.

It wouldn't matter if someone's grandpa was enslaved. Now that enslaved man's grandchild was legally equal. People would judge each other according to character, intelligence and talent, not skin color. As long as we were all equal, what could race have to do with it?

In the white world of Bowdoin I did what a white liberal was supposed to do: I attended the right symposiums, saw the right films, and discussed every racial issue, from apartheid to campus discrimination, in every forum I could find. I was the white man you could count on. Like any white liberal, I loved the "cool" that came in breezy conversations about how to bring the races together.

My only problem was that sometimes I ran into black students who demanded that we take the conversation deeper. One was a guy named Harold. Harold was a black freshman living among the whites in my dorm. I was glad to have him there. I would've been glad to have any Black there. Living in the same dorm with an African American was my generation's proof that things had changed. The policies and laws enacted during the '60s were finally having their effect. The races were living together right there in my dorm.

I knew this wasn't the end of the fight. A long road lay ahead. A few unreconstructed segregationists still roamed the land. Skinheads still scrawled racial slurs on subway walls, but weren't these mere echoes of the past? Of course they were. Now our future was clear. The last generation had shouted and marched, enduring beatings, jail and worse. They'd risked their lives to pass new laws guaranteeing equality. Now it was up to us to finish the job. That wouldn't be hard—not with black guys like Harold living right there in the building. Now that we were all on the same team it would be easy.

But Harold didn't see us as a team, and he didn't seem to think the road ahead would be easy. He talked as if racism was still around, and closer to home that most white people thought—white people like me. I should have found that challenging, but instead Harold's views only disturbed me. I wanted to be friends with him, or at least be his ally against the bad guys. When he treated me as if I were part of the problem I took it personally. How could he fail to recognize my empathy? After all, wasn't I free of the stain of racism? Couldn't I be part of his team?

Harold didn't think so. He talked about the gulf between his everyday existence and mine. I interrupted him with my white college boy's version of sharing. I interjected, misinterpreted, and revised what he was saying so it would fit with my self-absorbed viewpoint. I asked standard questions, paid little attention to his answers, and, when he didn't agree, I decided he was too angry to see the problem rationally. I did what we whites have always done—I dismissed, diminished, and devalued his positions. I failed to respect not only his opinions, but his knowledge. How did I know how other students were treating him? How did I know how the professors were reacting to him? Rather than validate his experiences, I made excuses for them.

It was something I would unwittingly repeat again and again with black people for the next fifteen years. I still cringe at the memory of my arrogance, but I know where it came from: denial. How could I possibly be a racist? I wanted Blacks to be equal to me, on my terms.

Harold was a black acquaintance, not a close friend. With only a handful of Blacks in a student body of well over a thousand, opportunities for real black-white friendships were limited. It wasn't until later, when I was captain of Bowdoin's swim team, that I met Jeff. He was a freshman from Harlem who was trying out for the team. Many away-from-home college students experience initial homesickness, or that fish-out-of-water sense that comes with unfamiliar people and places. For an African American from Harlem thrown into the virtually all-white world of Maine, it was much more than that. When the door opened admitting Jeff to Bowdoin, it revealed a long row of other doors still closed to him. At first I didn't notice that. Instead I saw Jeff the same way I'd seen Harold: a connection that was just plain "cool." The more we hung out together, the more I could see myself as a true liberal with a real black friend. I liked that.

Though I was always aware of Jeff's being black, I saw my friendship with him as having nothing to do with race. We shared the usual college men's interests in swimming, basketball, football, and women. Wasn't that enough? Unlike Harold, Jeff didn't immediately challenge me. He didn't have to. Jeff's skin color drew reactions from others, highlighting their racist attitudes. I had always denied the presence of some of those attitudes—at least in myself—while being totally unaware of others.

One thing I noticed was that whites presumed Jeff must be there on a scholarship he didn't earn. He was black, so he must have special help. Whenever an African American breaks barriers, or reaches a position formerly reserved for whites, whether it be a spot on a major league roster, or a slot in an exclusive college, we assume they're benefiting from two things: special help and lowered standards. At Bowdoin we saw this need for special assistance as a group characteristic of Blacks, and we identified Jeff more as a group member than as an individual. This group identity was in evidence whenever coaches and professors called Jeff "Jimmy." Jimmy was another African American on the campus. The mistaken identity might've been understandable if it had happened once or twice. It didn't. To many of these progressive educators black men like Jeff and Jimmy were interchangeable. Later I realize that this is a common problem among us whites – that we don't see Blacks as individuals, only as a group.

Jeff sometimes talked about white attitudes, but as I

witnessed how people treated Jeff, more often I saw those attitudes demonstrated right in front of me. At first I went through the same denial I'd exercised when talking to Harold, but this time I was dealing with a man who was willing to see if we could be friends. As the evidence of racism mounted my denials took on a hollow ring. And since I knew I shared some of those beliefs, could my indictment be very far behind?

Sometimes the evidence was inside me, emerging in small incidents that illustrated larger principles. When "Roots" came on TV Jeff and I watched the early episodes together. As we talked about what we'd seen, Jeff opened a window on a different view of American history than any I'd ever experienced. Through him I learned some of the background to the slave trade, how it destroyed families, ripping people from their homes, heritage, and lineage. Jeff told me that slavery hadn't just stripped people of their freedom, it also stole their language, and even their religious beliefs. He noted how many of these same processes were still at work in late-20th century South Africa. Apartheid based its social system on the principle that African ancestry was inferior. Our own college had a significant part of its endowment invested in companies operating in South Africa. This was a connection I understood.

One night, as I sat alone watching the end of one of the later "Roots" episodes, a preview of the next one came on. One snippet of a scene showed "Roots" author, Alex Haley, conducting an interview with one of his subjects. The dramatized moment was obviously pivotal enough to include in the trailer, which made me wonder why Haley was playing himself. Obviously this important role required the skills of a real actor.

When I discussed this with Jeff he corrected me. "That's not Haley," he said. "That's James Earl Jones. He's one of the best actors working today." When Jeff started naming a few of Jones's other roles I felt embarrassed by my own ignorance. Here was one of the most celebrated actors of our time, a man who'd played King Lear, Malcolm X, and the Jack Johnson part in "The Great White Hope." I'd seen him act before, yet I hadn't recognized him in the role of Haley. I felt as if I'd joined those whites who were always calling Jeff "Jimmy."

In moments like these I began to sense the deficiencies in my own knowledge. Jeff didn't always throw this stuff in my face. He just let it happen, then answered my questions. His answers often put familiar situations in a whole new light. Without knowing it, I was learning about my own racism. And Jeff was my teacher...

+ + +

My attitudes then were no different than those of many well-meaning whites today. We say we've conquered our racism, and we believe it. We make black acquaintances, work with black colleagues, and some of us might count one or two African Americans as casual friends. We are repulsed by the "n" word. We know racism exists, but we're sure it has ebbed. We might give lip service to ideas like affirmative action, but deep down we wonder if such things are really necessary anymore. We raise our children to practice "color-blindness" in their day-to-day lives. We might even encourage them to invite an occasional black classmate or friend to come by and play.

The idea of "color-blind" is one of the most important building blocks in our huge wall of denial. We like to say that we don't care what color someone is. In race relations this is the big lie. And it's demeaning. We aren't really blind. We see all the colors, and pay attention to them. We don't have to deny someone's color in order to see that they are there. Our color is an essential characteristic, and there's no reason to disrespect someone by denying it to them. Imagine telling your wife, mother, or daughter that you don't see her as a woman. How would she like that? Yet we think that denying an African American's skin color is a great way to neutralize racism. The truth is that it's a demonstration of racism.

Consider it from a white perspective: Does being white matter? Does anything in white culture matter? Do our parents and grandparents matter? How about our immigrant ancestors? If we want to be color-blind we must start with our own lives and histories. That reveals some discrepancies. For instance, why did our white great-grandparents get off the boat and start looking for jobs, when those black immigrants began work right away? Why were our white ancestors always struggling to buy a farm or start a business, when those African Americans were guaranteed lifetime employment? See where "color-blind" takes us? With a few perfectly logical steps we can eliminate the whole history of slavery. Now that's denial!

We live in a world that's almost entirely white. It might not seem that way because most of us can cite a few African American influences in our lives. I might like rap music and you might enjoy soul food. But ask yourself this: are those influences prominent because they are so few? Or are they basic building blocks in your worldview?

White racism still thrives in the roots of our society. While the idea of eliminating it quickly or entirely is not realistic, it should be possible to tremendously reduce it. Our two most essential tools are an honest desire to do so, and open minds. Our greatest obstacle is our own denial.

+ + +

How prevalent is racism? How deep do we have to dig to find it? Not far. It's near the surface, and down to the bone. It can be easily compared to sexism. It has a similar dynamic. Sexism is about differences. So is racism. Sexism is about power. Racism is too. Sexism is about superiority. Ditto racism. Some men assume that they have a right to demand obedience from their wives. In such a man's workplace a woman had better be subservient.

I See Color

This comparison isn't perfect. As a rule white women weren't brought here in chains. Even in the early days certain professions, such as teaching and nursing, were open to them. Their commitments as mothers and wives gave them a certain social standing. Still, if whites honestly examine their feelings and attitudes about sexism it opens a window onto the nature of racism. They are both all about who does the work, and who gets the benefit.

Many of us honestly want to put racism behind us. We want to do it individually, and we want to help society to do it. What's hard is finding that open mind. We want it to be there, ready-made. We want to think of ourselves as objective judges who will let the chips fall where they may. Anything less is unacceptable. Yet we subconsciously accept our own racism every day. We don't mean to. In the larger sense we don't want to. But in dozens of small ways we display white racism. We might call Jeff "Jimmy" or act on assumptions that we've never even thought to examine. Without thinking about it we regard race from a perspective of power. Whites define the way race works in America, leaving Blacks to choose between acceptance, resistance, or withdrawal.

So how did we blind ourselves to one of our most obvious characteristics? We did it with an exercise in Orwellian doublethink: we advocated one idea while living another. We put racial equality into our laws and court decisions, and put our children into nearly all-white private schools or virtually all-white suburban public schools. When Blacks moved in, we moved out. We seldom moved "because of race." We moved for positive reasons: the new house was closer to that private school, or was a better commute, or had more land. Or, if race was a factor, it was someone else's racism—maybe those "racist" realtors who wanted lots of easy home sales with commissions.

Yet somehow, despite our best intentions, we're still racists. Why? Because we don't believe we are. Our denial is built into our lives and culture. It's there in our whole approach. How can we hope to change something when we won't even admit that it's there?

Change isn't easy. It requires far more than lip service. It only comes when we search our own souls, accept whatever we find, and do the difficult work of getting rid of the old, and creating something new. We accept equality in theory. Yes, we say, two people, each with a different skin color, are equal. That's what we said when we "gave" Blacks all those rights in the '60s.

Back in those days we were strong on theory. When it was time to pass a law promoting equality, we were there. When it was time to obey the letter of the law we were close by. But when it came to act in the true spirit of the equality we were often absent. When we saw a few black males coming our way we crossed the street. When we saw a lot of black kids transferring to our children's school we looked for a "better" school. When several black families bought houses on our block, we moved. We looked at a lot of houses, some in "nice" neighborhoods, and others in marginal areas. We finally bought one in a "nice" neighborhood. It went without saying that all the "nice" neighborhoods were white.

In every instance we've avoided the real questions: Who are black Americans, and how did they get to this juncture? Who are we, the white Americans, and how did we arrive at our attitudes? How can we live together? How can we work, play and learn together? How do we find a way to truly care about each other?

We've been asking these questions for centuries. That's our tradition. But questions are supposed to lead to another tradition: that of answers.

+ + +

In the course of my adult life I've committed myself to

certain choices: allegiance to black friends, love for a black woman, and, eventually, marriage to her, and the sharing of parenthood for our child. As I made the effort to break away from the racial attitudes of my normal white background, I had to rethink everything I knew about race and race relations.

I grew up harboring conscious and unconscious racist beliefs. My family seldom talked about race. We didn't see any reason to. We lived in a community with very few Blacks, and supported businesses and institutions that catered almost exclusively to whites. As I got older, I moved toward eliminating my conscious racist beliefs.

Now, after 30 years of actively trying to reduce my racism, I can tell you something about this lifelong process. My hope is that you will be able to learn from experience, and create the tools to carry on this quest yourself. I realize that many aren't blessed with black friends and family members to guide you, but if you accept the truths my family and friends have taught me, you can succeed. Though you might not live in the same house with African Americans, or even in an integrated neighborhood, you can still learn to raise your children in a non-racist way. The first step is opening your mind to change, and examining your own denial. The best way to do that is to learn how being African American affects the way a person looks at the world.

If you want to learn, and truly desire to understand the racism within yourself, facing your denial is the first and most essential step. Once you do it, you can learn a new way of looking at everyday life. Then you can apply this to habits, relationships, and child-rearing. Once the process passes down through a generation your success will multiply, and you will have sown the seeds of a better future for us all. But you must take that first step.

The Man in the Mirror

The Process in Brief:

1. An open heart and mind: Drop the denial.

2. Letting go of old attitudes and beliefs.

3. Seeking out information and knowledge on race relations from those affected by it most: African Americans.

4. Implementing what we learn.

5. Through it all, we must have patience, persistence, practice and perseverance to be successful.

Chapter Three

◆

Racism Unplugged

rac-ism n. 1. The belief that a particular race is superior to others.
2. Discrimination based on race.

—The American Heritage Dictionary

In America racism is always the color of white.

I've learned this the hard way more than once. Though I am white, and I could easily go through life without ever facing the effects of racism, circumstance, and my own choices, have put me in situations where I've felt its sting. My wife, Danielle, is of African ancestry, and I am father to our daughter, Alicia, who shares in her mother's heritage. My life with them has brought racism home in a personal way, but even before I met Danielle, I'd begun to experience home-gown racism in ways I'd never imagined.

Thirty-five years ago, when I was first dating a black woman, I wanted her to come to Thanksgiving dinner at my home. (This was before I began dating Danielle.) I was still living under my parents' roof, so I had to clear any Thanksgiving guests with them. The idea of a young black woman sharing our family's Thanksgiving meal didn't set well with my father. When I brought it up he refused to allow it, out of "respect for the family." He felt that this was something I would understand. I didn't. When I pressed him on it he threatened to throw me out of the house. That morning I left for work wondering if I could come back home that night. If the woman I was dating wasn't welcome there, how could I remain? I'd come up against the question of race in the American family. Is it any wonder that the one American war where fathers fought sons and brothers battled brothers, had race at its core?

My father's brother defused this explosive situation. Recognizing that the repercussions were just too great, he persuaded my father to allow my girlfriend to eat at our holiday table. My mom's brother wasn't quite as open-minded. He told her he would break his son's legs if he ever brought a black girl home. In this poisoned atmosphere my girlfriend and I ate a Thanksgiving dinner together at my parents' table.

My grandfather was another story. He and I had always been close. My grandfather owned a gas station in New Haven. I worked there through high school and college. It was the kind of place that had a lot of regulars, and friends dropping in. It was a true "melting pot" of people. For a kid it was a natural magnet. The place had the kind of camaraderie natural to neighborhood businesses, but it also had a pecking order. A kid might have easily mistaken that as "natural" too. If a black customer drove in wanting only a few bucks worth of gas, he was presumed to be lazy, and almost certainly on welfare, but a white man buying the same quantity got his windshield cleaned. My grandfather had his buddies come in, sit down, and make their visits into a social call. Many of them worked for the oil company next door. One black man who was often around never seemed to be part of the conversation. Looking back on it later, I realized I'd never seen him in the same light as my grandfather's other friends. We all regarded him as someone on the outside looking in, almost like a cardboard cut-out of a man.

When I grew up, and started dating a black woman, my grandfather was the one who took it hardest. He cut me off cold.

"He won't even speak to me," I said to my dad.

"He's old school," Dad said. "He told me he'd feel the same way if you were dating a cow."

Racism Unplugged

Despite this insult, one day I went by my grandparents' home to try to explain it to him. He and my grandmother sat and listened as I made my case.

"She's smart, educated with a Master's Degree—all the things a family could want in a girl," I said.

My grandmother gave a tentative smile. (Years later, after my grandfather died, she would say to me: "I don't care if she's green, as long as she makes you happy.") Suddenly my grandfather rose from his chair and left the room. The gesture had the feel of finality. My grandmother had tears in her eyes as she struggled for an explanation.

"It's so foreign to him," she muttered.

In the years before my grandfather died he softened enough to speak to me again, but it was clear that things would never be the same. As far as I know he carried his attitudes with him to the end.

My father managed to swallow the idea of his son going out with a black girl, and when I continued doing it, his attitudes softened. Not long after that, when my girlfriend's car broke down at our house, my father looked at it, identified the problem, bought the parts, and repaired it right there in our driveway. It was the beginning of a difficult conversion for him, one that is never complete, but like anyone else trying to recover from racism, he has worked at it.

Such changes are rare. In the following years I learned what my black friends had always known: that racism is America's elephant in the living room. Racial hostility permeates attitudes, trumping all common sense, but we only speak of it when we absolutely must. This is true in my family, just as it is in many others. Eventually I started dating my future wife, Danielle, and our relationship deepened. After we married, Danielle and I managed a modicum of peace with my family, but it was far from perfect. Also, we still had to handle the hostility of the larger world outside.

Just before we got married, when Danielle moved from Ohio to my home state of Connecticut, it was my job to find her a reasonably priced apartment in a safe neighborhood. I saw this as a straightforward task, and I had what seemed like a reasonable amount of time to do it. I understood that race might be a factor, but I felt confident that I would find a nice place soon enough. In white-based circumstances the greatest challenge would've been finding the apartment where she would be happiest: a quest for the perfect place. Instead I quickly learned that I would be lucky to find her anything at all. It's not that there was any shortage of apartments; it was simply a matter of race. No one wanted to rent to a well-educated, conscientious woman who could pay the rent—at least, not if she was black.

One Italian realtor agreed to be frank with me because I was a "paisan." He couldn't do it, he said, because he would never rent to "a Shaniqua. Yeah, you know what I mean..." Unfortunately I did. At another place I walked through the apartment with the landlord, agreed on rent and a security deposit, and I actually reached the point of putting two thousand dollars in cash on his kitchen table. As we talked he told me how he'd just thrown out three college fraternity students who'd nearly wrecked the place. They'd left him with a damaged unit, and stiffed him on some rent. Up to that point I hadn't mentioned my girlfriend's race, but I guess something raised his suspicions. As he followed me to the front door, he finally asked straight out whether she was black.

As if to soften the question with a mystical touch, he said: "My wife had a dream that she was."

"Yes," I said. "She's a black woman with a Master's degree and a well-paying job with the State of Connecticut."

As soon as the words were out of my mouth he started back toward the kitchen. "You stay right there," he said. As he returned holding the two thousand in cash in his outstretched hand, he said: "Okay, I know you're a lawyer, and maybe you'll try to take me to court on this, but I'm not going to rent to your girlfriend."

I felt numb as I took the bills from him. Two thousand dollars is a lot of money, but it wasn't enough to make this man reconsider his racism. He was willing to let young white men tear his property to pieces before he'd rent to a well-educated, gainfully employed black woman. And I said that to him. I looked at that pile of cash, and thought of what money can buy, and what it can't. I felt physically weak. As a man I should've been able to protect Danielle from attacks. I should've been able to provide a roof over her head. I had no illusions: his racism was an attack on her, denying her a place to live. I felt like going back in and threatening him with legal action. That's what the law was for, right?

Danielle's reaction was more subdued. "If he's that kind of landlord why would I want to live there?"

"Don't you want to file a complaint?" I asked. "What he's doing is illegal."

"No," she said. "We just have to find a place. I don't want to waste time on him."

I reacted the way I did because I wasn't used to it. Danielle was. African Americans face this kind of racism every day. They know that they must pick and choose their fights or they'd be fighting every day of their lives. Often their white tormentors are open about it. Other times they hide behind any excuse that's handy. Either way the effect is the same: an African American is cheated out of something because of race.

Why do whites feel this way? One reason is that we've been taught to. We've learned racism from our parents, who learned it from their parents, and so on down the line. It's a worldview that carries all the way back to Columbus, and beyond. Some of it may have its roots in the casual brutality of white European culture. Long before Europeans started conquering the world, they went after each other. Tribes fought tribes, towns battled towns, and nations warred with nations. Europe didn't have a monopoly on organized violence, but they did seem to take to it far more readily than peoples on other continents.

In other parts of the world most evidence points to the exceptional nature of large-scale violence. In Europe it was the rule. In other cultures, people quickly tired of battle, negotiating peaceful solutions before they reached the point of completely destroying each other. European history often seems like an unending parade of massacres, and wars that only stopped with the last man standing. These brutal traditions paved the way for the Middle Passage, lynchings, and the Klan. The ideas underpinning those traditions live on in the virulent racial "theories" of militias and white supremacist groups.

What I faced in that apartment search wasn't as horrific a threat as a noose or a burning cross, but it was a harsh education. It reinforced my realization that what Blacks had been telling me throughout my life was an accurate description of their reality. Many white people say (and believe) that African Americans need only to claim their rights and equality will automatically follow. They think that black people expect a free lunch, and get angry when it's not given to them. In that moment, with the Italian realtor's rejection still ringing in my ears, I understood the difference between guaranteeing rights in a statute, and claiming those rights in the real world. As I walked away with that two thousand dollars festering in my pocket, shame, anger, and confusion combined into a terrible, empty feeling of helplessness. That's what the naked face of racism had done to me in just a few minutes. What was it like to deal with it every day? What was it like to know that there was no escape?

+ + +

As we examine racism we're bound to make errors of

perception. That goes with being white. If our examination arises from a genuine desire to do better, we're likely to grasp at whatever solutions seem obvious.

Busing has been a racial issue, here in New England and throughout the country, for more than four decades. It began as a tool for school integration in the 1960s. In many states the 1954 Supreme Court decision to integrate schools had been virtually ignored. Most public schools drew their students from nearby neighborhoods. If the neighborhood was white, there was no integration. To solve this judges were ordering black children to be bused to white schools and vice-versa. I thought this made sense. If white children were exposed to black children at an early age, maybe racism wouldn't take hold.

I trumpeted that position in a speech I gave at a high school for Black History Month in the late 1980s. Upon reading my speech, my close friend, Mike gave me another point of view. When I asked him why an African American would oppose busing he said: "Because of safety and their education."

"But that's what all those white parents are worried about. They think black kids will come in there and beat up and rob their kids... or worse."

"I know they do," said Mike, "but the real issues are: first, the safety of the black kids. You take a few eight-year-old black children, put them in a classroom full of whites, and the whites aren't in danger. They just think they're threatened because they've been brought up to think that way. But threatened children lash out. Those white kids are going to go after the black students. They'll push them, shove them, call them the 'n' word, and subject them to all the tortures kids are capable of—but always with a racist angle."

I nodded. "That makes it pretty hard to go in there that first day."

"And it doesn't stop," Mike said. "There might be some ebb-and-flow, but they just keep doing it. And it's not just the kids.

The parent of a black child has to worry just as much about white teachers. That's the second issue. What are they going to teach? That slavery was benign? That a black child can be equal if he or she will just act like all their white classmates? If the black child gets a bad grade are they going to recommend some tutoring, like they would with a white kid, or is it going to be a recommendation for transfer into a special ed program? Will they label the child as 'dumb?' That can destroy a child. That's why a lot of black parents would try to pull their kids out of public school rather than see them bussed into some all-white neighborhood."

Mike was being logical, yet his argument surprised me. I was far too accustomed to seeing the world through white eyes. When our daughter, Alicia, started at an almost all-white public school I learned this the hard way.

It wouldn't be the last time my dear friend was right when I thought he was wrong.

+ + +

Racism often seems like a grim American birthright. Some white babies in affluent homes learn it in the cradle, watching how their parents condescend to African American domestic workers. Other white children learn the "n" word before they hear African Americans referred to in any other way.

Many black children experience racism before they can form conscious memories. It happens in the hospital where they're born, or in a car, or on the street with parents or siblings. It might be an epithet or a personal encounter. Toddlers watch TV, hear the radio, and many have contact with the Internet. All forms of mass media, from talk radio to Saturday morning cartoons, are infected by racism. By the time an American child is old enough to understand the dictionary definition of racism, he or she has usually seen it, been a victim of it, or even practiced it, often without even knowing what it is.

Racism Unplugged

This is the kind of racism that falls beyond the reach of legal remedies. It is bred into the heart of the individual, and the culture of the society. In the 1990s, three decades after broad-based federal civil rights legislation, and four decades after the Supreme Court ruled segregation in schools to be illegal, I began to see how this problem works from a more personal vantage point. My African-American daughter, Alicia, started attending a suburban public grammar school here in Connecticut. The school was in a virtually all-white town, and its student population was a reflection of that. Alicia was one of a very few black children enrolled there. Her difficulties started immediately.

The first problem came from the children around her. We've all heard it said that children can be cruel, and when white kids meet black kids, that cruelty often shows itself in overt racism. Our daughter was subjected to racial taunts and slurs on a daily basis. When we complained to white administrators, their first defense was denial. Children make things up, and children misinterpret, they told us.

While there's no denying that children imagine things, those taunts were just as real as the Confederate flag displayed in the school's library. We didn't imagine that flag. The national symbol of African American enslavement was displayed among other flags, with no sense of its history, and no explanation for what it means today. The banner embraced by the Ku Klux Klan and the Aryan Nation—a flag often flown alongside the Nazi flag—was shown on an equal footing with our own Old Glory. When we spoke to the school authorities they saw nothing wrong with this. The flag was simply one more artifact from of our heritage, its meaning neutralized by time. Ignoring the flag's present-day symbolism, they could not admit that showcasing it without comment was an insult to the memory of all who'd lived in slavery, and their descendants. We kept up our complaints, but their draconian solution showed the poverty of their thinking: They removed all the flags.

Forty-five years ago many public schools began to schedule activities related to the study of Black history throughout the month of February. In a short time February became recognized throughout the U.S. and Canada as Black History Month. A quarter century later, when Danielle and I asked school officials about any programs that might educate children about African Americans, diversity, or anything that might come under that umbrella, they proudly pointed to their plan for a Roberto Clemente week. Roberto Clemente was a great baseball player in the 1960s and 1970s. He came from Puerto Rico, and did humanitarian work, mostly in Central America. He died in 1973 in a plane crash while on a mission to help earthquake victims in Nicaragua. But for all his qualities, I doubt that even he would have claimed to represent the whole of history of African Americans. That claim was left to the authorities at Alicia's school to make. They seemed to think that honoring Clemente covered the subject.

When faced with individual racist situations whites often feel that all-or-nothing is the only solution. When school districts had difficulty integrating due to housing patterns, we brought in buses. Administrators worked overtime to make sure every school had the right ratio of whites-to-Blacks. It didn't matter if children had to spend hours on the bus each day. What mattered was the racial math. It had to be right everywhere. A similar mentality went into the removal of all the flags at Alicia's school—if one had to go, they all went. When that mentality kicks into reverse it reduces any notice of racial issues to a minimum. That's how we wind up using a long-dead sports star to cover the history of a whole race—an approach that's very close to nothing.

Though racism is huge, permeating every part of society, it's also individual, and often subtle. I saw an example of this subtlety when the teachers at Alicia's public school decided that she needed special attention.

Despite taunts and racial slurs, Alicia was passing her classes. Her marks didn't put her on the honor roll, but they did show that she could handle the work. With a little more attention and encouragement from the school, we were certain our daughter could excel, but her teachers didn't see it that way. They saw a black child with a couple of below-par grades, and to them that meant one thing: our daughter had learning disabilities. They suggested putting her in a Special Ed program.

Special Education programs are at the heart of our society's efforts to give extra help to students who have particular learning disabilities. These problems are supposed to be diagnosed with some degree of precision: dyslexia, dysgraphia, or any of a wide range of hyperactive conditions, such as ADD and ADHD. Many people, including educators, have an incomplete knowledge of Special Ed and the problems it addresses. When they run into something they can't or won't identify, they use Special Ed as a catchall solution. When faced with a child suffering from the emotional toll of racism, Alicia's teachers' reaction was to deny the racism, ignore her potential, and focus on a symptom they thought they understood: schoolwork. Though Alicia was passing everything, her grades in some subjects were poor, and, of course, there were those emotional difficulties—difficulties that, in their eyes, must come from within her, and not from any external source in the school. So they suggested we put her in a Special Education program. That way they could deal with her "learning disability."

Her teachers had diagnosed a disability that simply wasn't there, while flatly denying the problem that was there. Why? For these white educators it was easier to believe that a black child had a substandard intellect, than to accept the notion that the white children might be racist. They had done their paperwork, filled out the forms, and all we had to do was sign off on the deal.

We didn't accept their conclusions, and rather than put Alicia in Special Ed we changed schools. We enrolled her at a Catholic school with a more integrated student population, and a somewhat less oppressive approach. There she eventually made friends, both black and white, and achieved honors.

The Catholic school was more open, but they had their own interesting educational conflicts. One difficulty arose when students and teachers talked about the pictures of Christ hanging on the walls. These images matched the Christ figures on the crucifixes, in the sculptures, and in just about every rendering of Christ in every Catholic school everywhere—the standard kind of pictures most of us knew growing up. Kids in Catholic schools see them in their classrooms daily, and Protestants find them everywhere from prayer books to Sunday Schools. This general image of a white Christ is also standard in other depictions from Hollywood movies to Madison Avenue ads. The public face of Christ as put forth by the whole of Western culture is that of a white man with long, straight brown hair. He looks a lot like a hippie.

But is that really what he looked like? In Roman times there were several sects of Jews, their skin tones varying from bronze to black. Some were as light-skinned as Arabs (not all that light), while others were as black as the Ethiopians to the south—obviously African. When Herod sent out his soldiers to eliminate the new Savior by killing every child under two years of age, Joseph, Mary and Jesus fled to Egypt (Matthew 2:13-20). All the lands around them were under Roman rule, so they might have fled anywhere, but most likely they would've picked a hiding place where they could fit in undetected. Egypt's people were mainly black-skinned Africans, so it is likely that Jesus and his family were the same. In Revelations Jesus' hair is described as being like wool, and his feet are referred to as "bronze" or "burnt brass." The Bible says little else that would indicate Jesus' race, but what is there goes directly against the notion that he was Caucasian.

Alicia's teachers were uncomfortable with the idea of a black Jesus. One teacher simply said they weren't going to address that question. The school authorities seemed more comfortable with a white Son of God who looked a lot more like a hippie than an African.

The Catholic School also had an American history text that described the Southern plantations before the Civil War as benign institutions which were "self-sufficient" neighborhoods where the Africans could get all that they needed. Had my daughter been white I probably wouldn't have heard much about this, but when your African American daughter is being told by her textbook that the enslavement of her race wasn't such a difficult thing, it changes the way you view her education. The downplaying and outright denial of the horrors slavery isn't just a grammar school problem. Consider this passage:

As far as physical conditions of life were concerned, the slaves were about as well off as most members of the world's laboring population... Although the slave worked hard, beginning with lighter tasks as a child, his workday was no longer than that of the Northern farmer or laborer. He was given time off to hunt and fish, and he attended the church and some of the social festivities of his white family.

That's from "A History of the United States" co-authored by T. Harry Williams, one of the 20th Century America's most respected liberal historians. It is one of the most widely used college histories of the past half century, and is cited in a 2010 Wikipedia article as a "standard textbook still utilized in American history survey courses." Even now in the classrooms of our most respected universities my daughter would be faced with the same kind of cultural apartheid she experienced in the backward texts of a Catholic grammar school in the mid-1990s.

+ + +

I See Color

If school had been the only place where Alicia faced racial problems, growing up would've been easier for her. It would have been better for me if I could've educated my own family and friends to the point where they would wholeheartedly accept her. But how many white families get that kind of education? Not many. My father and mother don't consciously practice racism, nor do my siblings, yet having a family member who is father to a black daughter has revealed racial fault lines among them that I'd never dreamed were there.

The racism my daughter endured from school and family was an everyday event with everyday effects—a constant drumbeat. It led to moments like one when I found her lying in bed crying. When I asked her what was wrong she said she was crying because she knew she could never get her wish. What was she wishing for? To be blonde and white. After all, isn't that the ideal set forth for every girl in our culture? Isn't that the same cultural ideal that insists on Jesus being a white man? How could he be anything else? Isn't that blonde child the one who should be sitting at Thanksgiving dinner? Or coming down the steps at school? Isn't that the kind of girl who gets a teacher's special attention instead of Special Ed?

Many whites hear these complaints and ask: "What's the big deal?" They wonder why anyone would worry about a flag, an image, or a few paragraphs in a history book. A part of that comes from the simple fact of dominance. In America whites have ruled for 400 years. While one of the aftereffects of the Civil Rights Movement is the tendency of many whites to think of ourselves as "suffering" from affirmative action, quotas, and other remedial programs, the fact of the matter is: we still rule. We still get the best jobs at the best pay. We own the vast majority (a majority far greater than our actual proportion in population) of banks, buildings, land, stock shares, government bonds, and so on down the line. We worship in expensive, beautifully designed churches, while many black congregations must settle for storefronts. We dominate television, radio, the Internet, and movies. Blacks get a couple of cable networks. We recently elected our first African American president to head a government run by a majority of white bureaucrats.

When you run just about everything, and you have always run just about everything, it's easy to forget the people whose blood, sweat and tears built so much of everything. Whites have spent centuries building systems of control. We like to think of those systems as beneficial to all. But when those systems tell a ten-year-old black girl she must accept a white version of everything, from faith to flags to history, it matters. That's when issues of law, economics and education touch individual people. That is when racism makes a little girl cry herself to sleep because she can't be the blonde, blue-eyed ideal formed from a thousand white lies.

Chapter Four

◆

Our Racism Is Not Their Prejudice

The obvious place to start with racism is one's self. With most whites this is a task of soul-searching requiring honesty, objectivity, and persistence. It never ends. It's also not just an introspective process. You can't seal yourself off from all contact, and think your way to a solution. When dealing with a subject as big, yet personal, as racism, experience is as important as thought. Your introspection must be matched by an effort to expand your horizons. Once you've faced your own racism, and opened yourself to African American history and culture, look at the whites around you. Are your children, or any of your siblings or other relations, ready to try something similar? Might any of your friends, neighbors, or co-workers be interested in exploring the issues of race? Can you share what you're learning with others? Are you having experiences, or are they experiencing anything, where race is a primary factor? If so then it might not take much effort to bring race into the conversation. Often it's already there.

But before we go further, understand this: racism is not prejudice. In America believing that one's race is superior to another, and practicing behaviors that enforce that belief, is specific to whites. Indeed, many Blacks may be prejudiced against whites. But the follow-up question to that is: Given their history and daily experiences why wouldn't they be?

The experiences that give us the most focus are the ones closest to home: situations and emotions that arise among family, friends, neighbors and co-workers. With any given circumstance, each individual involved can show us different facets of racism. For one person it might be a situation in the workplace. For another it might be a home sale in the next block over. Spouses, siblings, parents, and friends might all look at the same racial circumstances and come up with different interpretations. Their differing views will show how racism infects each person according to his or her temperament and experience. You will also see what attitudes are common to all of us. Try to look at the situations objectively, and consider all viewpoints. If you ask your friends and relatives about racial matters, listen carefully to each answer. Understanding the motivations behind other peoples' racial attitudes can often help us recognize aspects of our own racism. We just have to be brave enough to uncover it.

I've learned a lot about racism from the differing attitudes in my own family, and sometimes from the evolution of an individual. I've already noted some changes in my father's viewpoint. I saw a different kind of evolution in my brother, Louie. Louie was gay, and knew a certain kind of prejudice first hand. A lot of us might think that a gay man of whatever color would automatically understand the pitfalls of racism, and would already be working on eliminating it from his attitudes and behavior. Yet when I first started dating black women I wondered if my brother would understand.

When I got into my first interracial relationship Louie didn't seem to mind at all. I was glad for that, but I soon got the feeling that his "understanding" was more like the old concept of "tolerance" than real acceptance. He didn't have a problem sitting down to a holiday dinner with a black woman. He didn't mind his brother dating one. But the idea of my getting serious about a black woman—of getting a black sister-in-law—required a little getting used-to. Louie didn't have much conscious racism, but, like most of us, there were all those unconscious racist tics that arise when the situation involves people we know and care about. Maybe the fact that I wasn't too serious about these women made it easier for Louie's thinking to evolve. Did his own situation as a member of a harassed minority help in this development? I think so. Discrimination on the basis of sexual orientation is not the same thing as racism, but some of the same functions are at work. My brother knew what it was like to be an outsider.

By the time I met Danielle, Louie had adjusted to the idea of my interracial dating better than most other members of my family, but did that extend to the prospect of a black woman marrying his brother? That was a bigger hurdle. In the end he did accept it, but not before overcoming an obstacle I hadn't expected. It came when I started dating my future wife. Even before he met Danielle, Louie knew I was serious about her. That was when the issue of black children came into our conversations. A black girlfriend? That was fine. A black wife? Louie thought that might be okay too. But what about a black child, or children? Something about the picture of his white brother with an African American child disturbed him.

Louie looked at me as his straight-arrow lawyer brother whose future was with the movers and shakers of the world. Louie had already decided that I would run for office some day, or be appointed to some position of influence and power. He was a lot more concerned for my "image" than I was. Louie imagined how my family would look in a news photo. He worried about all the white folks who would be turned off. He was anticipating one of those many faces of racism that I hadn't even considered. I knew interracial couples bothered some people, and I knew it could a tipping point in their opinions of me. Louie saw a facet of racism more subtle than that: some whites can accept the couple, but not the children. With these people tolerance fades the moment the interracial marriage involves kids. It was one of the most common laments I encountered with other whites. It's the point where their racism often erupts into total rejection. Louie recognized this, and talked to me about it. He framed it as a problem I might face one day, but I knew he was also revealing something of his own unconscious racism.

If that unconscious racism was there, it began to fade when he met Danielle. At that point his personal feelings trumped any racism he had. He and Danielle clicked immediately, and over time this grew into a deep bond. From then on Louie was on our side. As far as it went with Alicia, he was her uncle and she was his niece, and though they only knew each other for a few short years, they formed a close, loving bond. My daughter still talks of Louie over a decade after his death. In the 1990s my brother fell victim to HIV. In his last months Danielle was often there for him in the role of caregiver. The caring went both ways.

Louie's sexual orientation was another thing my family had to accept, and they did so relatively quickly. We'd grown up in a world where gay jokes and gay bashing were accepted practices. In some cases they were even encouraged. Homophobia was the rule, rather than the exception. On gay-straight issues my family wasn't any more prejudiced than many others; we were normal for that time and place. In the 1960s and 1970s prejudice concerning sexual orientation was the norm, so when we learned Louie was gay it was an adjustment. But he was our brother. We'd grown up in the same house, shared the same experiences, had the same memories, and for many years, when there was no overt issue of sexuality, we'd just thought of Louie as Louie.

Like many American families, we learned the hard way that a HIV diagnosis brings gay issues directly into the spotlight. It's then that we learn who can accept a person's sexual orientation, and who cannot. When Louie was diagnosed all of us worked our way beyond whatever phobias remained, and we supported our brother as he struggled against a disease that he hoped wouldn't kill him. That support was a reason to be proud of my family, but it is also a lesson about the difference between racism and other forms of discrimination.

As Americans we all share a long history of discrimination. Though our founding declaration stated all men were created equal, they weren't including women or black folks. In the Republic's first decades there wasn't even a semblance of equality among white men. Our attitudes, traditions, and laws created a system nearly as stratified as India's castes. Discriminatory practices in matters of gender, race, ethnicity and religion were a basic part of that system. Inequality flourished in law, finance, commerce, education, and many less formal social relationships. Ever since then we've been chasing equality. It's still out of reach.

One way we tried to deal with inequality was by changing the law. Americans used legislation and court rulings to get rid of many property barriers limiting voting and other rights of citizenship. Laws providing public schools and financial aid have lessened some of the inequities in education. Legal remedies have helped women gain their rights in education, employment and in voting. The Bill of Rights provided part of the legal framework for religious freedom, while later amendments, acts, and legal interpretations have opened up opportunities for African Americans, Native Americans, and many others. But the law is a poor tool for changing attitudes, behaviors and habits. That begins with the individual.

Racism is the most widespread form of discrimination. It's also unique. It shares the obviousness of sexism in that it often begins with sight. In most cases we can look at someone and know their sex and their race. If your immediate ancestors were white, you are white too. If you are a woman, that is usually obvious to others. This isn't as true of ethnic groups, and most faiths are made up of men and women of various complexions and features. An Italian might be blond, while a Swede might be swarthy. Jews are mistaken for Gentiles and vice-versa every day. A Muslim might be black, white, or any other skin tone.

We might work side-by-side with a person for years and never know their faith or nationality. But we usually know their race.

While women face discrimination, they are also members of the family—every family. Even if a gay couple marries and adopts a male child, all three of them have mothers. Whatever the effects of sexism are on any given individual, women are there in every life in a very personal way. They cannot be avoided.

That's not true of Blacks. Many of us whites go through our daily lives without seeing many black people. Most whites live separately from Blacks because we want it that way. Why wouldn't we? White neighborhoods have higher real estate values, better schools, and better public services, don't they? We certainly seem to think so. Many of us accept integration in theory, but in practice we prefer caution, patience, and ultimately separation. In the end that means keeping white neighborhoods white. This self-enforced separation creates inequalities in everything from net worth to the price of groceries.

Back in the mid-1980s, when open housing laws had already been in place for nearly two decades, I was vice chairman of the Planning and Zoning Commission in my very white Connecticut town. Our town bordered one of the state's largest cities, and that city was home to a significant African American community. A vote was coming up on a proposed low-cost housing project in our town. Like most such projects, it would've provided decent homes and apartments for people who didn't have much money.

The town's Mayor was an old friend of my father's, and of our whole family. He and my dad had known each other for most of their lives. He had his own nickname for Dad, calling him "Doc." They lunched together every week, and once a year they went hunting in Maine. At the Mayor's request my dad had served on various commissions, and he often sought Dad's input on political matters.

The Mayor was a nice guy, warm, and usually positive. When I was just starting my career he had helped me. After I finished law school he steered clients my way, and it was he who appointed me to Planning and Zoning. One morning he found me in City Hall reviewing applications the Commission would take up at our next meeting. The low-cost housing was on his mind.

"You can't vote for that project," he said.

"Why not?"

"It's no good. If they build here, it'll bring in the Blacks, and that won't help at all."

"How can you be sure?" I asked.

"Are you kidding? Look, I know we aren't supposed to be racists here, but what I'm saying here isn't really about race. I have no problem at all with some black people, but this project is aimed at bringing in too many of them, and these aren't the Blacks who pay their way either. These are all those drug addicts on welfare from the city, ones who are moving from places they already trashed. They aren't like us. We've got a good town, and we don't need those kinds of problems, so just do me a favor: think about it, and I'll bet you'll see what's right."

"So I should vote to keep the Blacks out."

"You should vote to keep crime out, and drugs out. Vote to keep them out, and make our streets and schools safe. That's what I'm saying."

I could see this conversation was a dead-end. I was up against a man who wouldn't admit to himself, or anyone else, that he was a racist. In most instances he would never need to. He didn't think of himself as a racist. He was the mayor of a white town, and white towns were safer, more solid... better. He worked in a city hall that was nearly all white, and to him that made it a better city hall. His children went to white schools, he and his family shopped in stores with white clienteles, and he belonged to white clubs. Why? Because it was better to be white than black, and everybody knew it, consciously and subconsciously. Did he ever deal with black people? Probably. He might see a few at political functions, or do business with them whenever he visited the state capital up in Hartford. He might've employed black service personnel to clean his house or tend his yard. I'm sure he'd never been a member of any group formally dedicated to white supremacy. He didn't need to be. He had a whole social structure on his side.

The Mayor's racism wasn't virulent; it was practically benign if that's possible. White was all he knew. To him Blacks occupied a separate world. He lived in a community where whites sat at the head of nearly every table. His support of implicit segregation policies was ingrained and automatic. Like every other white person, when he pictured a mugging, the mugger was black. To him prostitution was a bling-bedecked black pimp with an all-black roster of drugged, diseased women. When he visualized black children coming into a school, he probably saw graffiti, guns, and illiterate high school graduates. Racism ruled his limited imagination, leaving him unable to see African Americans as real people. To him Blacks were just a special interest group he didn't want to serve.

The Mayor's request was a product the racist beliefs he'd grown up with, but that was only a part of the problem. His was not simply prejudice, for that is a pre-conceived attitude about people, places, or things that may be based upon prior experience or no experience at all. But it doesn't contain racism's notion of superiority. The Mayor had his prejudices, but they wouldn't have meant much if his belief hadn't been backed up by his political power. The Mayor was a public official. The law gave him the authority to influence legislation, law enforcement, funding, and the allocation of public resources. Though he didn't change my vote, he knew that others would be more compliant, allowing him to bypass people like me.

Our Racism Is Not Their Prejudice

His efforts to block low-cost housing were based on reasoning akin to that of Jim Crow and Apartheid. Quite literally, he was keeping African Americans in their place.

I must note here that the Mayor was one of the kindest, gentlest people I've ever known, and he is still a beloved figure in our town. Despite these outstanding qualities, he also harbored racist beliefs. He was further proof that, while subconscious racism doesn't necessarily make us bad people, it does diminish us as individuals by robbing us of a part of our humanity.

This is one of the areas where racism differs from sexism or discrimination against gays and lesbians. While each has his or her own unique circumstances, people of different sexual orientation are already members of our families. They live in the same houses, go to the same schools, shop in the same stores, worship at the same churches, and swim in the same pools with their white relatives. Many white males are sexists, and homophobia infects whites of both sexes, but how can they avoid the subjects of their prejudice? If a white politician or businessman totally ignored either gays or women he would quickly see negative effects on his daily life. Yet cutting Blacks out of the loop is second nature to most of us. This gives racism an oppressive force beyond that of mere prejudice.

+ + +

Racism is the belief that race is a primary determinant of human traits and capacities and that racial differences produce an inherent superiority of a particular race...

—Wikipedia

I'd dated other black women before Danielle, but as Louie had noticed, none of those relationships had turned into anything permanent. Then one day I was standing by a swimming pool, and met my future wife. It was a close friend's wedding day, and Danielle's mother, Elaine, was performing the ceremony. Danielle and I started talking, and the next thing I knew I was going to visit her. I met her mother, and was impressed with her, but I was surprised by what Danielle said when we were alone.

"Mom doesn't want me dating white guys," she said. "It's a matter of trust."

"She can't trust me?"

"She's not sure. She wants to have lunch with you."

"Just with me?"

"Just with you."

So I made a lunch date with Elaine. I was pretty nervous going in, and she had plenty of questions for me. When I realized I had some answers for her concerns, I began to relax. As our lunch progressed her questioning turned into conversation, and we got along fine. She liked me and I liked her.

Many white people would label her distrust "reverse racism." It wasn't. My future mother-in-law's concerns came from the prejudice produced by years of experience. She knew quite personally the mistreatment Blacks suffer at the hands of whites. In America today a black woman can't practice racism toward a white man. She might not like him, and she might even dislike the whole white race, but for her racism isn't an option. Besides, unlike my friend, the Mayor, whose sense of superiority was so deep that it was almost invisible, Elaine felt no superiority. She just wanted to be sure her daughter wasn't going to get hurt. She wanted assurance that I would respect Danielle. She needed to know that I wasn't a typical white man who was ignorant about the complex issues of race.

Before you can practice racism, you have to be able to oppress the race you're targeting. To do that, you have to be a part of the race in power. That power has to be there in a general sense, even if it's less obvious, or neutralized in the individual circumstance. Recall my experience trying to get

Danielle an apartment. Or my ability to deny someone a job in my law firm due to race.

I was white, Elaine was black. She had a great deal of influence over the woman I wanted to date. I knew that, and it gave her power. Her distrust of me was rooted in the fact that I was white. She'd lived her whole life in a society where whites rule. Whites own the banks, the businesses, and the institutions. Whites run Washington, New York, Hollywood, and almost all the major conduits for news, entertainment, and communication. Elaine had grown up in a world where the preferences of whites limited the places where she could live, the schools she could send her daughter to, the churches where she might worship, and the whole landscape of her daily life. Over the years she'd seen that equation of power shift a little, but not a lot. Whites held the keys then, just as we do now. She could never escape that fact. It was in this context that she distrusted me.

I was a young white lawyer. I could live wherever I wanted, in whatever way I wanted. As long as I stayed within the law, my only limitations were those of ability, ambition, and imagination. If I didn't like black people I could, with minimal effort, insulate myself from them and much of their culture. I would never feel oppressed by black people or by the black race as a whole. In any given circumstance I might feel thwarted, stymied, frustrated or disturbed. A black person might hurt me or even kill me. But America's culture, society, government and business were on my side. Going beyond that lunch, and using any broader measure, I was the one with power on my side. As a young white lawyer I had all that... and I wanted to date her daughter. Who could blame her for distrusting me a little... and still she was willing to invite me to lunch!

She was willing to do much more than that. She was ready to listen. When she asked me questions she paid attention to my answers. She let me say whatever I had to say, and responded politely, agreeably, then warmly. Her distrust was of the white man she didn't know. She didn't regard my white skin as a plus, but she didn't hold it against me either. When it came to my race, she had reservations. Reservations are not racism. They are fears, questions, or concerns. In this case they were concerns born of experience. She simply wanted to get to know this young man who wanted to go out with her daughter. She wanted to make sure I was all right.

Some of you might downplay those larger contexts, and argue that she was being racist. After all, in this instance she was the one with the influence and power. But her concern was not that I was inferior. She wanted to be certain that the man her daughter was seeing wasn't unaware of racism, or of the day-to-day difficulties Blacks face. Though she distrusted whites as a whole, she was willing to give me this opportunity so she could hear me out. She allowed me the chance to win her trust. She asked her questions, and I answered. In time we built on that. Two years later, when I married Danielle, her mom became "Mom" to me too. She trusted me enough to bless my marriage to her daughter. She continued to give me her trust, love and affection for two decades, right up to the day she died. And I relied upon her sage advice for life's most important decisions. None of that is racism.

Chapter Five

◆

I'm OK, You're OK

pa·ter·nal·ism, n. the system, principle, or practice of managing or governing individuals, businesses, nations, etc. in the manner of a father dealing benevolently and often intrusively with his children.

—Random House Webster's Dictionary, 2002

Ever since the first time a white European enslaved a black African, the more benevolent whites have sought to soothe racism's sting by portraying it as a family affair. Enslaved Africans were children to the Great White Father, and he would see to it that they suffered no harm. White protectors would shield Blacks from bigotry, violence, and hardship. Many benign slaveholders also would have said they were saving black laborers from irritations such as knowledge, idleness, and false hope. They would allow their captive workers the simple pleasures of song, dance, and laughter, while protecting them from disturbing outside influences. That was a core plantation myth.

The myth changed with the times. With the Civil War and emancipation, plantation owners gave way to landlords, foremen, religious and civil authorities, and teachers. Whites owned, Blacks rented; whites hired, Blacks worked; whites sermonized, Blacks worshipped; whites taught, Blacks learned. With slavery officially over, this attitude created a one-way street of racism.

One reason we could be so benevolent was our numbers. There were more of us than there were of them, especially in institutions of power and privilege. That was certainly true when I started at Bowdoin College in the 1970s. Even as recently as 2009 only 3.2% of Bowdoin's first year students were black.* Thirty years earlier there were only a fraction of that—so few that they might've rightly seen themselves as tokens.

Bowdoin had a long history of giving lip service to racial equality. The College had graduated its first black student in 1826, and from that time forward Bowdoin had a policy of admitting a few of the black students who qualified. Over the next a century-and-a-half a smattering of African Americans went through the college, learning whatever their white professors taught them. If they also learned that these whites saw them as nothing more than children, they must have kept it to themselves. But by the time I got to Bowdoin this was changing.

When I was there some black students were demanding that we take conversations about race to a deeper level. One of these students was Harold, the black man living in my dorm, who I wrote about in Chapter One. In the dorm Harold was the lone Black among many whites—clearly a token. Earlier I wrote of my own psychological deafness when talking with Harold: how I failed to hear anything that didn't fit my preconceptions. Was I ready to talk about race at a deeper level? Harold was about to find out.

Harold acted on the demand for real dialogue by starting a conversation in print. He wrote an article for a campus publication indicting well-intentioned whites for their attitudes toward, and treatment of, Blacks. On a surface level I might have known that he was talking about people like me. In a deeper sense I had no idea what he was saying. I read his article, told myself I liked it, then sat down with him at dinner. I wanted him to know that he'd done the right thing. I wanted

---

* from: *The Bowdoin Orient*, April 2, 2010, "Decade in Review: Diversity on Campus" by Will Jacob and Gemma Longhorn

him to see that there was light at the end of the tunnel—that even though other white teachers and students hadn't figured it out yet, I had. I understood. I felt his pain. I wanted to help him and his people get the rights they so richly deserved. With all the desperate desire of a well-meaning liberal, I wanted him to know that I heard him, and I cared.

Harold wasn't impressed, but he knew he was the one who'd started this dialogue, and, in doing so, he would have to listen to responses he didn't like. He was used to that. Harold had been hearing, seeing, and sensing things he didn't like all his life, especially in the realm of race. So he engaged me by trying to explain the gulf between his everyday existence and mine.

I was surprised. I hadn't expected anything negative from him. I'd assumed Harold would be glad to have an ally. Here I was, ready, willing and able to do all I could to secure Harold's rights and privileges, and all he wanted to do was take me to task for it. As he compared the details of our lives I tried to steer the conversation back to what I thought to be its proper course. I wanted to tell him all about what I could do for him. I interrupted, interjected, and talked over his arguments, trying to reshape his ideas so they would look like mine. I failed. Naturally, I blamed my failure on Harold. What was wrong with this guy? Here I was, solidly on his side, and all he wanted to do was carp on the negatives. How could he expect to get anywhere without people like me? Like many whites before and after, I looked at this angry black man, and assumed his anger was simply an irrational loss of control—a temper tantrum. It would take me decades to see in myself what Harold already recognized: I was treating him like a child. I wouldn't validate his experiences or his oppression.

Think about it. How many times do Blacks tell Jews what is or isn't anti-Semitic? Would any of us allow "outsiders" to dictate the discussion on what constitutes anti-Italian, anti-Irish, or anti-German bigotry? Yet when it comes to the racism against Blacks, we not only enter into the conversation, we define and control the discussion itself! We don't allow them even the "privilege" of defining their own oppression.

Recall Jeff, who we also met in Chapter One. Jeff was my first real African American friend. Jeff and I talked about racial issues, but, as with Harold, there was only so much I was willing to hear. As I listened to Jeff, and observed his life on campus, I began to recognize that some attitudes, practices and policies I'd always regarded as neutral were actually racist.

This was a big step, and didn't come easily. Finally I was learning about the language, gestures, and customs of racism, and my friendship with Jeff was allowing me to see it from a black point of view. I couldn't be black, but if I empathized with my friend, I could begin to imagine some parts of what Blacks experience with white folks. I was beginning to learn that if I was going to understand how life worked for African Americans, I was going to have to exercise my imagination. I don't mean that in the sense of making things up. I mean looking at white people treating my friend in a certain way, then allowing myself to imagine how that worked. It wasn't just the treatment itself; it was all the circumstances surrounding it. If someone with power and influence disrespected me because of my Italian ancestry I would have options. I could go to someone else with equal or greater power. I could call in a cop or authority figure to mediate. If it happened during a commercial transaction I could go to another merchant, or make a public stink in front of other patrons.

Jeff's options were far more limited. If he went around one person, the next person he would deal with would probably be white too, and might be less inclined to intervene simply because the racial issue was present. Other authority figures would feel the same constraints. In a commercial transaction in a white establishment a complaining black person is almost always seen as "playing the race card." The complaint might be heard, and even acted on, but that black person knows he or she will be even less welcome in this store in the future.

I'd never had to use my imagination this way. I'd grown up in the white world where civility and respect were built into every encounter. Anything less is an affront. But when Jeff described his day-to-day life I began to see that different rules applied. At first I resisted his descriptions. For every one of his complaints I found a benign answer. For every slight I saw a legitimate excuse. White girls on campus didn't really fear him. He was wrong about being invisible to white professors and coaches. The campus cops didn't really stop him more often, or watch him more carefully. They stopped us all and watched us all equally. I was sure of it.

But the sheer quantity and quality of episodes eroded all my explanations. Eventually my denials weakened. On campus I would see him walking toward me, and notice the white girls looking away. I would listen as he talked to a professor, and realize the man was operating under the assumption that Jeff had come to Bowdoin on some kind of free ticket—probably taking the place of a qualified white. (Jeff was an honors pre-med student.) I clung to my excuses for as long as I could, but like old clothes, they got raggedy. After awhile I realized that none of my white friends got that kind of treatment. When a teacher condescended to a white student it was always for individual reasons pertinent to that particular situation. When they did it to Jeff it was standard procedure—one size fits all. Each instance was a glimpse into the paternal elements that lie at the heart of so much unconscious racism- seeing African Americans as a group, not as individuals.

Jeff told me challenging truths, but he seldom challenged me personally. We were friends, and he probably thought that might change if he went too far. But the bigger reason might have been the amount of energy necessary for such an effort. Jeff would describe incidents of racism in his everyday life, but he didn't try to explain their root causes. It would be easy to assume he wasn't aware of them, but I think he knew. What's far more likely is that he simply didn't want to go there. Getting me to accept the facts of unequal treatment was hard enough. Bringing me to a full understanding of why those facts existed would have been just plain exhausting. Jeff let me stumble on in my ignorance because he didn't have the energy to constantly educate me. Showing me all the nuances of my own racism would have been a full time job. Jeff had classes to go to, work to do, and goals to pursue. It was not his job; nor is it the responsibility of Blacks to educate us.

It took years for me to learn the everyday consequences of racism. It was only when I married, became a father, and was fortunate to have a black best friend, that I began to connect the dots. Being black in America means dealing with inequality all day every day. When white people see you walk in a room, your race is their first impression. When you walk into a store, the white owner and salespeople will focus on you, and even feel threatened, because of your race. When you go out to hail a cab, your race becomes an issue. When you sit down in a restaurant, your race will affect the service, almost always negatively. These things might not apply to African American businesses and people, but that just means that in a limited number of situations you'll be treated as an equal—the way white people get treated every day. When you deal with a white you can count on some degree of pity, condescension, distrust, or outright hostility—the various faces of racism.

So shouldn't whites be concerned? Shouldn't we act? Not if we're acting in order to help our poor, put-upon black brethren. Not if we assume that they need our help more than we need theirs. Not if we're doing it because we feel sorry for them. That's when we display the paternal face of racism. It shares the same root as Kipling's "white man's burden" and the "duty" to lift up our "little black brothers." When we approach our relationships with African Americans with any subconscious notion of "helping those less fortunate" we prove the point Eldridge Cleaver made when he told whites: If you aren't part of the solution, you're part of the problem.

For centuries progressive whites saw paternalism as a valid approach to race relations. Abolitionists wanted to "grant" enslaved Blacks their freedom. After Abraham Lincoln acted to fulfill this dream, whites called him "The Great Emancipator." Harry Truman "gave" African American men equality in the armed services. As Chief Justice of our nation's highest court, Earl Warren "gave" black children equality in the classroom. Lyndon Johnson made a gift of equal access to public facilities, then followed up with the right to vote and "open" housing. Each of these actions had a worthwhile goal. None of those goals have been reached. Racism still plays a role—often a decisive one—in schools, ballot boxes, housing, and the military. White business owners discourage black consumers, white teachers condescend to black students, and white bureaucrats create obstacles for black constituents.

Paternalism may be the most prevalent form of unconscious racism. It goes hand-in-hand with Liberalism. It often comes with good intentions, but underlying those intentions is the subliminal feeling that Blacks simply can't cut it without our help. For many of us whites it's something we sense, but refuse to identify. For Blacks it's one of the many white attitudes and behaviors that's just plain tiring. We can't be taught anything if we're unwilling to learn.

+++

Some years ago I wrote a series of op-ed articles for my local paper about issues rooted in racism. I addressed integration of schools and housing, studies in black history, and the differences between racism and other forms of discrimination. The articles didn't make me popular, but they did draw some attention to me and my opinions. It seemed as if the most positive reactions came from white groups whose purpose was to deal with issues of racism.

There are many such groups in almost every American city. Sometimes they spring up from a real, recognized need. Others begin in response to an event or situation arising between Blacks and whites. It might be a chance altercation between police and citizens, or a racial incident in a classroom. Other times it's more about commerce than authority: a white storeowner versus black clientele, or white neighbors against black neighbors. The spark ignites a conflict. Suddenly everyone sees there's some sort of trouble, and the one clear cause is race. The fire is contained, but the embers still smolder. Black folks turn inward to their own community to heal their wounds. White folks aren't sure what to make of it, but some of the well-meaning among us develop an unquenchable thirst for helping. So we start a group.

Some groups meet and talk, and a few progress to action. These groups are mostly white, affluent and liberal. Usually one of their most prominent claims is color-blindness. They usually see themselves as dealing with a problem that goes both ways. They regard black distrust and animosity toward white people as "reverse racism." They want to solve that too.

These well-meaning whites want to solve the problem without ever taking real responsibility for it. They avoid any possibility of self-indictment and sidestep evidence of hard feelings. They're more comfortable with the notion that there is no right or wrong, just opinions that must be respected. Today most of the progressives who join such groups feel that they have moved from the naïve liberalism of the 1960s to the fulfillment of one of the great liberal American dreams: the election of a black President. Though most of them have learned that America's racial problems won't fade with a single law or election, they always find a way to believe that we're almost there. One more step, one more speech, one more generation, one more program, and we'll get to complete equality.

This isolated optimism leads them into strange logic. Often when they hear about an affirmative action program, they wonder whether it might be another example of "reverse racism." They sometimes see such programs as tools for making things easier for Blacks in the job market, guaranteeing them preference over whites. The concerned white liberal might contend that "in reality" and "in the long run" this hurts the cause of equality. They argue that if race plays a role in a Black being hired instead of a qualified white then the black worker must not have the proper skills. Inevitably this favored Black will display incompetence, and the employer will decide: "I won't make the mistake of hiring one of them again." The white liberal will recognize that the affirmative action was there to solve a problem, but, as he or she sees it, the solution simply isn't realistic. Blacks should work their way up through the ranks just like the rest of us did. But are "qualifications" something that can be measured with exactitude? Imagine being judged on these qualifications by people who don't believe, respect, or even like you. Their assessments of you become the measuring stick for getting an education or for obtaining gainful employment.

White liberals will usually accept without question the employer's verdict about the black worker's performance. They don't probe or question. After all, it's common sense, right? Using race as a criterion for hiring doesn't work. Competence is the only test, and if the white is competent, then the white should get the job. Good as that might sound, it leaves many questions unanswered. Did the black employee have the skills? Did doing the job require cooperation and acceptance from white co-workers? Did they give it? And even if the difficulties with the black employee are legitimate, is that a good reason for the boss to decide not to hire other black employees?

I See Color

We regard African Americans as being separate in a way that we never saw immigrants from Italy, Ireland, Greece, or any other European nation. If we give black culture any credence, it's only in "giving" them the right to have it. If they want to study their history, that's fine. We tend to doubt that they have much history. After all, what did Africa ever do but get itself colonized? They apply this attitude to the present as well as the past. Let black folks study their own culture and history, but when they want to enter our world, they must study our life.

White educators will contend that in the halls of academia all knowledge is equal. That means that in the big picture we must put black history in its proper place: an isolated continent peopled by primitive cultures whose influence on the grand scheme of things was limited at best. To them African thought could never compete in the marketplace of ideas. These educators don't consider that before 1492 the best-educated European had no more influence on his world than a respected village chief in Kenya had on his. The only concern for white educators is which culture predominated in the marketplace of blood and iron. Without even thinking about it, white educators heed the dictum: Those who win the battles write the history. Teachers follow this dictum by erasing African culture from the books. White educators accept the notion that Blacks must assimilate. If they want to enter our world, they have to leave their paltry culture and nonexistent history behind.

These beliefs are usually unconscious. We learn them early on by implicit, and at times, explicit, methods. The most common method is exclusion, or the complete absence of respect and knowledge about black contributions. The best way to identify them is to look at peoples' actions, and often at their inaction too. I witnessed a telling example of this some years back, not long after one of my op-ed articles appeared in my hometown newspaper. A group called LEAP contacted me.

They had space in a neighborhood center right by a housing project where they ran an outreach program. They'd been there for a couple of years, developing programs to tutor kids in reading, math, theatre and many other areas. They worked with "inner city" youth after school and in the summers.

I'd been writing about racism's effects in several areas including education. Some people from LEAP read my articles, and invited me to take a look at what they were doing. I went, hoping to find a good program.

My guide that day was the program's director, and with us was the instructor to interns. They gave me a tour of the place, outlining the possibilities a child would have for learning, play, and entertainment. It was clear that their programs were created to closely parallel what these children were learning in school. If a young boy was having trouble in math, there was someone here to help him. If a little girl's problems with reading were being ignored in the classroom, someone here could get her started. All in all it seemed to be a sincere attempt to address that neighborhood's problems with youth and academic achievement.

As we walked through the rooms, stopping here and there to watch the activities, we were joined by a couple of college-age interns. These were the young people who volunteered to oversee groups and individuals in the various programs. At this point I noticed a curious form of segregation: many of us were white; all the young volunteers were black.

I'd seen this plenty of times before, and, at that moment, I thought of it more as an observation than anything else. This was the way it always happened: Earnest white liberals band together to help the people of the "inner city." Some young whites come to these jobs with the best intentions, and a few are open enough to take advantage of the unique education this experience provides. Those few get an inkling of the paternalism inherent in the process.

The LEAP staffers were certainly earnest and well-intentioned. When we stopped in their media room, they proudly displayed of some of the educational materials they'd managed to get people to donate. There were shelves of books and videotapes, as well as equipment for putting on shows. That summer they were particularly proud of a contribution from filmmaker, Spike Lee.

"We have an original draft of one of his screenplays," the Director told me.

"Really?" I said. "Which one?"

"It's that one…" He looked up at the shelf, and took down the script. Glancing at the cover he said: "It's 'Do the Right Thing.' We're going to have the kids put it on it as a play."

"Wow," I said, trying to picture how they would adapt Lee's story of violent racial conflict to the stage. The kids we'd been observing were mostly elementary-through-middle-school age, with some high school students. I knew the movie, and thought that having children of those ages perform it as a play would be adventurous to say the least. How would they handle the riot? The fire? And all that language? I assumed they'd thought these things through. "That may be my favorite Spike Lee movie," I said. "That'll be quite something, turning it into a play, don't you think?"

It took a few seconds for me to notice that a silence had fallen.

Finally the director admitted: "Yes, well, I'll admit, I haven't seen the film." He glanced at his colleagues. Each one looked around at the others, then at the floor. "Yes, I'm sure we'll be looking into that," one of them said.

It was a single instant in a much larger story. I was there that day, but I would soon be gone. They would be free of my questions, but they'd revealed a troubling ignorance.

I don't know if they ever performed "Do the Right Thing," or if so, whether they did the story justice. What I could see was that these sincere whites had managed to start an educational program, locate it in an appropriate place, gather materials, put together a staff, bring in kids, and yet none of the staffers, administrators or volunteers had bothered to watch one of American cinema's classic films—maybe the best film ever made about racial tension. Even when they were given a special copy of the screenplay, they hadn't read it closely (if it all), nor had any of them bothered to rent the video. But it was good enough for their black students.

These white people had no intention of dissing one of the world's top filmmakers. Nor did they mean to ignore black culture in general. It just never occurred to them to watch the film, or to pay heed to most other details of African American culture. To them the black struggle to earn a place in American film was black actors getting the same roles as whites, or black directors putting out the same kind of Hollywood fare we've been watching for decades. They feel good whenever they see Morgan Freeman play the President, or even God, just as an earlier generation of liberal whites felt vindicated when Sidney Portier played a teacher, cop or lawyer. Those kinds of roles gave them evidence for the stale old white liberal argument that "race doesn't matter to us; in fact, we're color-blind."

But few whites go to black films. Many of the black actors and actresses we see in white-produced films play stereotypical roles. When you watch a new TV show or go to a newly released movie, analyze what roles the black actors and actresses are playing in them. And then ask yourself who chose them for that part. Most often the answer will be one of us

As a rule we don't read black historians or novelists. For centuries we've listened to black music, but once a black artist's songs got popular the recording industry made a point of churning out cover versions by acceptable white musicians and singers. As soon as these were available, we bought them. We prefer to remain in the comfort of our own white culture, and we've convinced ourselves that it's the broadest, most inclusive culture on the planet. But I wonder what Spike Lee would have said about that if he'd been standing next to me looking into those embarrassed white faces.

+ + +

I saw an example of the same attitude from a different angle when I observed a group meeting in a state-sponsored prejudice-reduction program called "Study Circles." This group was reading books about racial problems in schools, cities, and the marketplace. The first title that came to my attention was "Savage Inequalities" by Jonathan Kozol. When I saw the title I could make a pretty good guess that this was written by a white liberal. As I looked down the reading list I saw a long list of white authors. Some were Jewish, many were women, but hardly any were black.

"Why don't you read black authors?" I asked them.

They looked at me as if I'd introduced an entirely new idea. Some found it suspect. "But we're looking at inner city education, and these are the experts," said one woman.

"You're talking about educating black kids and reducing the racism in those schools, right?" I asked.

"Yes."

"And here in the prejudice-reduction program we're admitting that race plays a big part in the problem, right?"

"Yes."

"Then we're dealing with racism, specifically: white racism as it's practiced against black people. Let's look at it a different way. If we were talking about girls in the schools, and the topic was male sexism against women, would you only read male authors?"

"I—I guess not," said the woman.

"We'd be reading all women authors," another woman admitted. And they began to understand my point on a surface level. What was probably still beyond them was the fact that racism is so embedded in us that we practice it even when we think we are helping reduce it!

+ + +

Many of us grew up in a world where laws concerning race were going through a huge transformation. The laws changed faster than white attitudes or perceptions. When long-time segregationist, Lyndon Johnson, came around on civil rights, he fought hard for a statute outlawing discrimination in public facilities. These included restaurants, hotels, motels, theatres, and anywhere else that opened its doors to all comers.

While he was fighting for passage of the Civil Rights Act Johnson illustrated his reasons with a story. A black couple worked for his family, serving as maid and handyman in both the Johnson's Washington house and at the LBJ Ranch in Texas. A couple of times each year Johnson would ask this couple to transport one of his Cadillacs between Texas and Washington, while he and his family flew. At one point he learned that the couple was driving several hundred miles out of their way between Washington and the ranch. When Johnson asked the handyman why, he explained: they were more comfortable taking a northerly route to Illinois, then they would swing south toward Johnson City, Texas. That's the only way they could find a reasonable number of restaurants, motels, and rest facilities that allowed Blacks access.

Many years later my father and I were talking with my mother-in-law, when the conversation turned to past vacations and trips. My dad and Danielle's mom both had some warm memories of their respective vacations, but then my dad started telling us about some trips he'd taken through the South when he was younger. One of these was a train trip, and from my mother-in-law's comments it sounded as if she knew the route. She said: "Yes. I remember whenever we went down that way on the train I had to learn to hold it in. Often it was a long way between rest rooms."

My dad looked at her quizzically. "You were on the train?"

"Yes."

"But weren't there rest rooms onboard?"

She went on to reply that of course, there were, but she wasn't allowed to use them. Here was the disconnect between what we grew up with and what the black experience was at the time. He was of her generation, and they had both grown up in the same country. Yet they hadn't.

The proof that segregation made little impression on whites is evidenced by my father's memory. We don't even know when we're doing it. We're too well trained in our insensitivity. We've learned our blindness well. It's like breathing.

Most of us fail to learn about racism from observation because we don't have any context. When I went off to college the context of my life was that of a white family in a white neighborhood. My friends were white, my school was white, and our church had a white congregation. Bowdoin was more of the same. The Blacks I knew were exceptions.

My white friends didn't know any more about African American life than I did. They had the same context. To us the history of racism started with the evils of slavery. We'd been taught that those evils ended in a terrible civil war, but then the white south managed to extend racial discrimination with something called Jim Crow. Finally, after a long, painful struggle, the promise of freedom was redeemed in the civil rights laws of the sixties. We'd been raised in a majority culture that liked its history neat, clean, and comfortably progressive: a straight line drawn through centuries. This made for a story of American race relations that conveniently ended in the here-and-now with equality at hand. If there was anything left to do, it was only in the details.

But as the saying goes, the devil is in those details.

If we'd listened we might have learned something. Harold and Jeff might've told us about being late for work because a white cop decided they looked suspicious. We might've noticed how slow salesclerks were to wait on people like Harold and Jeff, if they got service at all. We could have recognized the instructor's assumption that any black student probably needed remedial reading, or the admissions counselor who automatically reached for financial aid forms the moment a black face came into view.

For all I know, Harold, Jeff, and the other black students did tell us those things. If so, we didn't hear them well enough to remember. Our ears were blocked by our own assumptions, and our memories suffer from our own limited experience. We rejected evidence automatically, and if we did hear an uncomfortable fact, we questioned its accuracy. We did this most often when faced with the different ways Blacks were treated simply because they were black.

It was especially hard for me when I thought I was being my "liberal best." Long after I'd graduated from law school, when I was just beginning to get into serious racial discussions, I spoke to a racially-mixed audience of 500 Connecticut high school students. I'd worked hard on my speech, and was proud of its insights. However, when I had my friend, Mike review it, he had criticisms. Though his criticisms were clear and constructive, I got defensive. I let all that go, and over time my friendship with Mike only got stronger, then a few years later I looked at the speech again. With time and experience I realized Mike was right about all of his points. As more years have passed I've learned to listen more carefully, probe, and reflect upon his points. If I give myself an opportunity to weigh and accept them, I usually see what he means.

For me this was the hardest part to swallow. Wasn't my opinion as valid as Mike's? Not if I was blindly accepting my race's excuses. Like so many whites, I resented any resistance to my efforts to be part of the solution. I wasn't being open to the possibility that I was wrong. What I came to see was that my opinions failed when set against Mike's experiences and knowledge. When it came to race, he was the teacher and I was the student. If we were going to be friends, I needed to give him that respect, and learn from him. That was the only way I would ever walk the walk.

Over time I recognized some of my misperceptions about race. One thing led to another, propelling me to question my attitudes and actions more directly. In any given situation—at a counter, in my car, in a classroom—I examined what was happening, then imagined it with all racial roles reversed. In my mind Blacks became whites and vice versa. When I did this I could see that many situations became unreal. When the hostess seated the white couple at the table by the picture window, I imagined the diners as black. Suddenly the scene didn't look normal. The same thing happened when I applied this to movie roles, or scenes on TV news reports. Whether I was looking at a crime story or an ad for used cars, race always changed the equation.

Once I developed this habit I began to connect what I was seeing with what African Americans were telling me. When I saw white store clerks monitor black patrons closely, I also noticed that it didn't happen to whites. From that I could see why a Black would have a much harder time getting a job there. If the store did hire a black person, he or she would be the last to get a promotion, and when layoff time came, the black clerk was more likely to get the axe. I saw this seemingly subtle racism (so subtle that whites totally miss it, yet so complete that it strips Blacks of respect, opportunities, and real material wealth) in commercial transactions, legal disputes, residential decisions, conversations, and almost every other area of day-to-day life. My white friends and I always got the kind of treatment that I'd been raised to see as "normal." Blacks were treated differently, which meant they were treated worse.

This ignorance can turn misunderstandings into insults, and well-meaning gestures into disasters. Whites who feel they are free of all racism often translate their supposed freedom into a benign arrogance. When we put this arrogance on display we're often surprised, angered, and disillusioned with the result.

One time Danielle and I had dinner with a white minister and his wife. The minister told us how he'd learned of a group of local black clergy who gathered once a month to discuss difficulties black families faced in their city. He found out where and when they met, and one night he decided to attend. "I wanted to reach out," he said. "After all, we have to build bridges." He went on to describe his amazement at their reception of him. He entered the meeting, made himself known, then told them he was there to help. The ministers didn't exactly jump at his offer. "I sensed a coldness," he said. "None of them welcomed me. None of them seemed all that interested in listening to me."

I glanced at Danielle, and knew she was thinking more than she was saying. At that point I spoke up: "Were you invited?" I asked.

"No," he said. "It was a meeting of ministers, so I thought, as a minister who was sympathetic to their cause, I would be welcome."

"Did you call or email any of them, or make any effort to notify them you were coming?"

"No. I didn't want to make a big deal of it. I just wanted to drop in and tell them a few things about what we might be able to do for them. They come from poor neighborhoods. We can offer them a helping hand, but only if they're willing to take it. How can they expect to get anywhere if they won't let others help them?"

"But you were dropping in uninvited at a regularly scheduled meeting that's generally known as one for black ministers there in the city. That's the description you'd heard?"

"Yes."

"And you had things you wanted to say."

"Of course. I wanted to bridge the chasm between our communities. What's wrong with that?"

"It's their meeting, not yours," I said. "They're talking about their congregations, not yours. As you say, they have problems. That's why they're meeting. They have to deal with joblessness, schools, transportation, health—all kinds of problems. Some are the same things you have to face, and some aren't. Either way, this is their meeting. They might want to sort things out, and figure out what they agree on, before they approach any outside agencies for help. They have resources of their own, and they might need to meet to discuss how to use those. They might have a thousand good reasons for not wanting a white outsider walking in. And one reason might be that no one invited you."

"I wasn't there to hurt them," he protested. "I wanted to build a bridge, but they wouldn't even hear me out."

"Being uninvited, once you were there, it might've been wiser to listen. It's partly an issue of trust, as well as you being part of the problem. You barged into their meeting, assuming they needed your help when they hadn't asked for it. Maybe they know how to save their neighborhoods, and maybe they want to get that done before they start building bridges out of those neighborhoods."

When Danielle agreed, the minister finally reconsidered his position. "I guess maybe I was barging in. That's not what I meant to do, but I see your point. You're right. I hadn't looked at it that way."

This minister was looking at the problem of race the same way most of us do in the white community. It's a problem we need to solve for them. It's not a problem we face every day. When we go in the bank or restaurant, we don't have to wonder how tellers or wait staff will react to our white faces. When our kids go to school, we don't worry about their teachers or classmates making an issue of their skin color.

But we are right when we think of racism as our problem. It's inside of us. We're the ones who are doing it, and often we're doing it without even knowing it. If we want to solve it we have to start with ourselves. When we sit down with Blacks we need to listen. As we listen, we need to imagine ourselves in the positions they describe. When I walk in a store, does the clerk behind the counter start watching me? When I go to the bank for a loan, do they look at me and immediately assume a low credit score? To really understand racism we have to make these comparisons habitual, and we have to be observant and imaginative. Watch interracial transactions carefully. Switch the roles, and see how it looks.

Malcolm X advised whites to go back to our own communities, and face the racism in ourselves. He could've added that we should keep our minds, eyes and ears wide open. We might be surprised at what we see.

Chapter Six

Blinded by the White

When I was a young lawyer I went to work for Harry Greenberg. Harry was Jewish, and was proud of his affiliation with a Democratic Party that had passed so much civil rights legislation. Many Americans see Harry's religion and his political party as progressive forces on issues of race. Harry had been the boss in his office for a quarter-century, and in that role he'd hired lawyers, clerks, and secretaries. When I came to work there all the employees were white.

It was a small firm, and at any given time there were only a three or four employees besides us. That might be why I didn't notice the uniformity of their skin color. Harry liked to think of himself as liberal. He made it clear that his goal was a color-blind world where someone's skin tone simply didn't matter. He would've been appalled to think that his hiring practices were racist. When the subject of race and hiring came up Harry would go out of his way to mention a black woman who'd been his secretary. The only problem was, she hadn't really been his secretary, at least not in the sense that he implied. He made it sound like he had hired her, paid her, and had her there in the office working exclusively for him. It wasn't true.

He was speaking of Mrs. Baker who'd served as secretary to several small law firms in the building. Her husband was an attorney in one of those firms, and she was a paralegal. I don't know of any substantial work she did for Harry. Maybe because he often mentioned her, or maybe because I had my own blind spots, I hadn't thought much about our employment policies until we needed to hire a new paralegal.

I See Color

In small law firms people share tasks, and often one job overlaps with another. Our new paralegal would be called on to perform some secretarial duties, act as messenger, and answer the phone in a professional manner. No matter how much schooling or training the candidate had, he or she would still be expected to sit at a desk near the elevator doors, typing, answering calls, and greeting clients and prospective clients as they first entered the office.

We had four candidates, all with paralegal credentials. If you rated all four on resumes, degrees and references, the two that would head the list were both black. I assumed we would want to hire one of these, but when I began talking to Harry I realized he had already ruled out both of them. His reasons were couched in professional terms. Could this one handle the files? Could that one deal with our more difficult clients? Was this one's school better than that one's? He never said a word about skin color. Had I asked him, I'm sure he would've claimed that race played no role in his considerations. He might have even persuaded himself of that.

In fact, race was the only factor. The next two candidates were white, and Harry seemed eager to hire one of them. Though their resumes couldn't match the first two, and their job experience didn't measure up, they were the right color. Suddenly these two less qualified candidates were the only pool we had. I protested, pointing to the better of the black applicants (and the best of the four). She had experience, skill, references, and a manner that suggested friendly competence. Still set on one of the white paralegals, Harry dismissed my comments. He wanted the white applicant.

"But she's never worked in this kind of office," I said.

"That doesn't matter," he replied. "I like her."

"But you have an applicant whose qualifications are damn near perfect," I said.

"It isn't all about diplomas and resumes," he countered.

Blinded by the White

"But look at the woman you're turning down," I said. "She's done the work, earned the recommendations, and she already knows the basics. You're saying that, even when we've got a chance to hire someone with excellent experience, we should go with the one who's straight out of school. We've had new paralegals before, Harry. We'll spend all our time training her."

"I think you're exaggerating," he said. "She's fresh. We won't have to train her out of a lot of bad habits."

"We need the best person we can find," I said.

"A lot goes into that," he said. "I've got to think about our clients. When new clients, or prospective clients come in here we want them to feel comfortable right away. Remember, hers is the first face they'll see when they get off the elevator. I've got to consider that. I don't want to send the wrong signal."

"And you're saying that a black face sends the wrong signal," I said.

"That might be a part of it," he admitted.

"It's that," I said. "You let your racism outweigh all those qualifications. It's ridiculous, and I won't be a part of it. If you hire her, I leave."

When all was said and done Harry came around and chose the black paralegal. After she had been with us for a while, Harry admitted that she was one of the best staffers he'd ever hired. Still, I had to wonder, how could a man whose background and inclinations were seemingly liberal and racially enlightened, act with such obvious racism when hiring "the first face they'll see?" He would, with no hint of irony, talk about how their family maid was "more like family" than an employee. Yet the few times I was at their house, she waited on us much in the same way servants did in the old movies of the '40s and '50s.

My boss had been hiring people for twenty-five years. Not one had been black—unless you count Mrs. Baker, who'd been chosen for him. If you asked him about it in a general way he would've denied that racism played any role in his hiring practices. In his own mind he had no doubts that his decisions were fair, and based purely on each applicant's qualifications. Yet, when judging between black excellence and white mediocrity he'd opted for mediocrity. This man who professed color-blindness had decided purely on the basis of color, while creating an excuse about appearances to hide his racism from everyone—including himself.

I had to wonder: Do we all do that? Do I do that?

Many whites profess to believe in a "color-blind" world whenever they are faced with affirmative action, or any other process that seems to favor black job applicants. They argue that it's wrong to favor anyone because of race. "Wasn't that what Dr. King's dream was all about?" they ask.

They sometimes cite the most famous passage of King's "I Have a Dream" speech. That day he said: "I have a dream that my four little children will one day live in a nation where they will not be judged by the color of their skin, but by the content of their character. " But he said much more than that. King also told white America: "[W]e've come to our nation's capital to cash a check. When the architects of our republic wrote... the Declaration of Independence, they were signing a promissory note to which every American was to fall heir. This note was a promise that all men - yes, black men as well as white men - would be guaranteed the unalienable rights of life, liberty, and the pursuit of happiness. It is obvious today that America has defaulted on this promissory note, insofar as her citizens of color are concerned. Instead of honoring this sacred obligation, America has given the Negro people a bad check, a check which has come back marked 'insufficient funds.'"

When our checks bounce we have to make good, and if the debt is owed by whites to Blacks, then color-blindness is not a payment option. It's just a way of declaring bankruptcy. We, the white people, owe black people freedom. It isn't ours to give. It's what we took, and now we have to return it, along with payment for the benefits we reaped from keeping them in bondage. Admitting their legal equality is a step toward that, but all we've really done is move up to the payment window. Now we have to come up with the tools and opportunities African Americans need for economic equality. Our forebears built the system to do two things: keep Blacks out of the mainstream of prosperity, but keep them close, so that they could perform the work we didn't care to do—American apartheid, or Jim Crow. "Color-blind" proponents maintain that all we have to do is allow Blacks in the door, just as we do whites. From there they are on their own.

The color-blind defense is noxious on two fronts. First, it's a lie; of course we see color. We always have and always will. We see race as the same way we see that someone is a woman or man, or if they have brown or blond hair, or if they're tall or short. Race is visible, so you have to be blind not to see it. Second, being blind to race is disrespectful. If I were to claim to be color-blind I would be telling my wife and daughter that, in order to actually see and accept them, their color would have to mean nothing to me. I would be denying an aspect of their identity that affects them every day. It would be like refusing to see my sister as a woman.

When we want new faces, we automatically look for faces like ours: white. Whenever we hire a white candidate, giving little or no consideration to black applicants, the debt increases. Paying it down requires an affirmative attitude and real action. A well-intentioned white trapped in this system has to try harder just to give a black job applicant a fair hearing. That's how the system is built.

When faced with a Harry Greenberg, and his urge to show prospective clients a white face, we must do what we can to counteract him. We might argue that a face of color will bring in new clients. We might show how other, more integrated firms have benefited. But if we close our eyes, and profess the principle of color-blindness, when we open them our world will be bleached white.

The alternative is a narrow, withering apathy. In the short term it's more comfortable, but in the long run it's debilitating and dangerous. When we learn to live with our racism we also learn to deny its existence. We forget those moments when we thought the black doctor was an orderly, or when our black co-worker walked in just as we were launching into a racial joke. Such moments rattle our nerves at first, but we get inured to it, then we forget we're even doing it. After all, we're not the ones who are offended. At some point we don't think about black peoples' professional standing, or racist punch lines, or the logic behind our hiring practices. We don't notice our own words and actions. When someone else notices, we say: "I don't care about race. Somebody can be black, white, or even green. It doesn't matter to me. I'm color-blind."

For the last century racial color-blindness has served as an excuse, goal, and basic principle of racial equality. "We must be color-blind." Congressmen say it, presidents cite it, and courts uphold it. We've heard it from teachers, clergymen, and our parents. "When I look at someone I don't see black or white." How many times have you heard a white person say that? And in almost any circumstance, if that same white describes an African American, it's likely the description will begin with the person's color. Bush and Clinton are presidents. Obama is a black president. Bill Gates and Warren Buffet are billionaires. Robert Johnson and Oprah are black billionaires.

We like the color-blind mantra because it's so easy. Whenever a racial problem threatens us, we trot out the idea that we don't even notice color. Once that's established, any outcome seems possible, including the one we want. Usually we want the outcome that's totally white.

The color-blind argument is often used to counter quotas and affirmative action. Opponents of these measures claim that any preference based on race is wrong. But are these preferences? Or are they simply ways to address the leftover racism that somehow survived all that color-blindness?

Harry was color-blind. Black, white, yellow, green—it was all the same to him. Yet he'd never hired a black person in his law firm in over 25 years. Nor would he close the firm in honor of Dr. Martin Luther King's holiday. With him it wasn't a decision; it was simply the way things were. To his mind he was no racist, but a few clients were, and it was important not to offend them. That meant keeping the staff white. Harry would've excused his hiring practices by playing the realist card: we all have our ideals, but business is business. A less appealing, but truer way to say it would have been: A white staff would attract a white clientele, and that's what we were after. Whites are the ones with money. Right?

What I'd done in getting Harry to hire a black paralegal was an exercise in affirmative action on a very small scale. Did we turn away a white person? Yes. Did a job formerly held by whites go to a black person? Yes. And what was the result? We hired the person with better credentials, and she was the best paralegal the firm had ever had. But if all a white person knew was that we'd had a white and a black, each with similar educations, the assumption would be that we hired the black candidate because she was black. Most whites would assume qualifications had little or nothing to do with it. And that would be reinforced if she failed.

This history repeated itself when we had to hire a new paralegal for the law firm I now own with my sister, Lynn. It came down to two women, one white and one black. The black woman, Tanya, didn't interview very well. She came across as being less interested than a job seeker should be. She did have important qualifications. She had graduated second in her class, and it was obvious she knew her way around the law and legal firms.

Laurie, the white applicant was more energetic, and she made a good impression on my sister. They seemed to have much in common. Lynn talked with Laurie at length, and said that they had "connected," but something about this applicant rubbed me the wrong way.

Though Lynn leaned toward Laurie, we still followed standard procedure, and called both candidates' references. Tanya's former employers had only good things to say. She was conscientious, efficient, honest and personable. Laurie's former boss had a different story. She'd wanted to fire Laurie. "I would've too," she said, "but my other paralegals might've rebelled. They didn't exactly stick up for Laurie, but they had a little sympathy because this was her internship, and they knew how hard it would be for her if she got fired. Other employers see failed internships as red flags. You're paying someone nothing, or next-to-nothing, and still you let them go. It doesn't look good. I knew Laurie wouldn't be around long, so I just did my best to avoid her. For the next couple of months I got to work each day, went straight to my office, and hid there. I was hiding from her."

Later, after we hired Tanya I asked her about her poor interview. "I'm sorry about that," she said. "I've interviewed at so many white law firms. No matter how well things went, or how good my references were, I never got the job. I've been out of school for a year. Many white members of my class got a job, but not me. I figured no white firm was ever going to hire me. You called me in for the interview, so I came, but I'll admit, that morning I wondered why I bothered. I guess that was on my mind."

We never heard from Laurie again, but she would've been a perfect candidate for the "a-Black-took-my-job" syndrome. Most of us have heard this chant many times. It's almost always blamed on a policy or mandate that's forcing the employer to hire incompetent Blacks in place of highly-trained whites. And it's usually a myth. Most Black-took-my-job scenarios look a lot like our choice between Laurie and Tanya—close calls at the end of a process where race played a role in the discussions, but the final decision was based on the needs of the work itself.

The other part of the affirmative action issue that doesn't get discussed or addressed is the "qualifications" label in general. If you are white and believe that racism still exists, imagine what Tanya had to go through before she ever applied for our paralegal position. Her road was loaded with the minefields of racism; Laura's wasn't. How many Blacks are eliminated early on in the educational, legal and employment processes, often by an unfair and ignorant evaluation of their qualifications? While Tanya was lucky to have instructors who graded her on her ability, what would her chances have been if her teachers hadn't liked her, and had graded her accordingly? The issue of qualifications can become a slippery slope, one that needs to be carefully analyzed in each situation.

When quotas and affirmative action get into the news it usually involves a large corporation, and a policy that affects many people. The corporation hires hundreds, or even thousands of new people every year. Its hiring practices are documented. The documents show a long history, and an accuser can use that history to demonstrate the effects of the company's hiring policies. Often there will be more than one accuser, and sometimes the ACLU, or some other concerned group, will provide free legal counsel. If the company won't comply with fair hiring practices, the matter goes to court, and gets into the news.

What slips between the cracks are all the small businesses out there. That's where most of the jobs are. When a white beauty shop owner won't hire an African-American she knows she's not likely to be sued for her hiring decisions. The same is true in many restaurants, retail stores, and other small enterprises. Most of them have only a few employees, and many haven't been open for more than a few years. That makes it almost impossible for plaintiffs to prove the patterns and intentions necessary for a successful discrimination suit. Even if they could prove it, there wouldn't be much money awarded, and the only employment practices that would change would be those in that particular company. The rest would keep hiring the same way, no matter what the courts rule. Employers know they're likely to get away with it. That makes lawsuits less likely. In the end, many white small businesses never hire Blacks.

Three reasons white people give for their race-based decisions are education, economics, and class. They use these excuses for covering up any racism their perspectives might reflect. "It's not race anymore," goes the argument. "It's prejudice against poverty. People are uncomfortable with Blacks and whites because they're poor." Or, "Blacks are behind in America because they don't have much education." The class-and-economics argument presumes racism would disappear if Blacks made more money. But take a moment and think of rich, powerful black folks, such as Oprah Winfrey and President Obama, who've been subjected to racism simply because they were black. The same is true with education. Famed historian and Harvard professor Dr. Henry Louis Gates, was arrested in his own home due entirely to his skin color. Any black man or black woman who's been stopped by the police can attest to their arresting officers' ignorance of their educational, professional or financial successes. Many cops assume a black person is poor, uneducated, and guilty of criminal conduct. Their dress, car, speech, and background don't matter. They are black, and that's enough. We whites insist that we act the way we do because Blacks are less educated or poorer. We say that we would accept them more readily if they would only pull themselves up by their bootstraps, and accomplish as much as we do.

Dr. Martin Luther King went through most of his life believing this. He thought if Blacks could gain the right education they would soon be on an equal footing with whites. Then racism's grip might ease. As he neared the end of his life he was deeply disappointed at the growing evidence that whites would never see Blacks as being good enough. King came to see that only a change in white attitudes would bring Blacks the respect they deserve.

We say we base our attitudes on the facts. We don't. We say our viewpoint has nothing to do with racism. It does. We select the facts we want, ignoring any that might prove us wrong. We see the black person who lies, cheats and steals, and don't notice the hundreds of black folks who do the right thing, because this fits into our predispositions about Blacks. But when white, mostly Jewish, investment bankers did the same things, we rightly did not prejudge or condemn all Jewish people.

We defend our attitudes from charges of racism by building a closed circle of assumptions. These arise from our seeing and believing without questioning. If you are black I might assume you are poorly educated. My assumption isn't based on racism. It's based on a clouded combination of economics, class and education. We learned to make these assumptions long ago, and we've never found reasons to question them. The few Blacks we meet or work with who don't fit into our view are seen as "exceptions." Indeed, how many Blacks have suffered through the indignity of having a white coworker tell them they were "different", not like other Blacks? These whites are ignoring the facts that stand right in front of them.

Once we accept one assumption all the others follow. What we hide from is the first assumption—the one underpinning all the others: Black is bad, white is good. Once this assumption is established the pieces of any argument fall into place. If he's black he must not be educated. If he's uneducated then he must be ignorant and illiterate. If he's ignorant and illiterate, then, if he gets any job, he'll get it because he's black. If she's black she must not be educated, so she must not be competent. If she's incompetent she must've gotten her job because she was black. We do this every day, often without even thinking. We make black people jump through hoops, often without even knowing that we're doing it. When someone points out what's really happening, we deny it. How could we be racist? It goes against all our assumptions.

African-Americans have to face this every day. They know that racism lies at the core of white folks' attitudes, but in an individual circumstance is the white person truly intending to be racist? Or is this just another instance of unconscious racism bred into the whole white society? Often they don't want to face these tiring questions, but if they want to get a certain job, or attract a particular client, or close an important deal, or even just pass through a checkpoint, they often have to figure out how much they can trust the white who holds the key. They need to know if that person truly hates them, or merely underrates them—or is it a little of both?

These questions and assumptions can manifest themselves in unexpected ways. Some years back my best friend, Mike, had reason to visit the Cheshire Juvenile Facility. At the time Mike was in his thirties. He'd earned a Master's Degree, then went back to school for his law degree, and was admitted to the bar. He'd been a lawyer for about three years. He was doing what most lawyers do at correctional facilities: meeting a client. But first he had to get in.

Keep in mind, this wasn't just anybody asking to see a prisoner; this was the prisoner's attorney. This is a role that's an essential part of our justice system under the Constitution. Mike was counsel for the defense and an officer of the court. He was dressed impeccably (as he always is) and his manner and demeanor were entirely professional.

That didn't matter to the people at the front desk. The

secretary and the guard, both white, were there to make sure all visitors were on the up-and-up, and they took it upon themselves to see Mike as a suspicious character. Once they decided this, they challenged him.

"If you're going to see the prisoner you'll need the right identification," said the guard.

"You've got it right there," Mike said, nodding toward the ID he had already set out in front of them. "My driver's license."

"Yes, but you're claiming to want to see him on a legal matter," said the secretary.

"Yes. It's about his case."

"Then we'll need proof that you're his lawyer."

Mike took a business card from his wallet, and set it next to his driver's license. "That should do it."

Both of them looked at the card. "No, I'm afraid we need more than that. Haven't you got something official, or maybe some paperwork from your office showing that you do represent the prisoner?"

"All you have to do is ask him."

"Right," said the guard, "but his say-so doesn't prove that you're really a lawyer. We'll need some documentation."

"Uh… I'm not sure what I can show you."

"You might start with your bar license," said the secretary.

"My bar license?"

"Yes. The license they gave you to practice law."

" I don't have anything like that on me," Mike said. "You don't really mean the license itself, do you?"

"That's what she asked for, isn't it?" the guard said.

Mike looked from one to the other. Neither of them appeared to be joking. At that point Mike thought he might blow a fuse, so he walked away. He needed to keep his cool, and he needed accurate information. Could they really demand to see his bar license? It didn't make sense. The young man he was visiting wasn't being held incommunicado. Other visitors didn't have to produce legal credentials. Most of them weren't even lawyers. In an effort to burn off steam and get the information he needed, Mike called me.

"Bob," he said. "I'm out here at Cheshire to see a client, but they won't let me in."

"Why not?" I asked.

"They say it's because I need to show them my bar license. Is that true? Can they demand that?"

"I'm not sure if they can," I replied, "but they never do. I've been practicing law for almost twenty years, and they've never asked me. Nor has any other lawyer told me they have. You're sure they want your bar license, and not some other kind of ID?"

"Yeah. I gave them my driver's license and business card, but they say I have to prove I'm a lawyer. What do they want? My bar license is just like yours—in a big frame on my office wall. Are they expecting me to bring that every time I come here?"

"That's ridiculous," I told him.

"I'm glad you said that. I thought it was too, but I needed a reality check. I'll talk to them, but if they stick to their guns, I might be calling you again in a few minutes."

"I'll be here," I said.

When he returned to the entrance a black guard was coming on duty, and the dynamic changed. This guard knew how things worked, and though he might not have been overly fond of lawyers, he didn't want any trouble—not from his coworkers or from Mike. "You go ahead and sign in," he said.

With that Mike was in. Later he told me all that had happened after we'd talked on the phone. It was one more instance of white folks making life a little more difficult for someone with black skin. Mike fights this battle every day along with every other professional African American. In white people's eyes black attorneys become defendants, black doctors become janitors, and black athletes become gang members. When we meet African Americans we automatically give them a big demotions, stripping them of years of schooling, degrees, and job experience.

No doubt the bureaucrats who tried to bully Mike created their own excuses, saying to themselves that something about him was suspicious. Such suspicions are the perfect cover for racism. If we asked them they would say that his suit wasn't right, or that he didn't act like a lawyer. They would call him uncooperative, belligerent, or just plain hostile. They would be angry at Mike's anger, resent his resentment, and if race came up, they would agree that race played a role, saying that his aggressive behavior was a textbook example of reverse racism. They would say it was their job to keep the prison secure, and to stop visitors who might be suspicious or hostile. Here was a hostile black man. Aren't they the most dangerous kind?

Their real reasons for stopping Mike were all rooted in race. As far as they were concerned the problem was in the behavior of the African American lawyer who would not do everything they required him to do. After all, they needed to make sure that he was an attorney and not someone sneaking in to assist a jailbird. Black attorneys were somewhat of a rarity and he wasn't about to "pull rank" on them. To them this black lawyer was claiming the same rights as a white one. That needed to be corrected.

Mike was dealing with a clerical worker and a guard. One might guess that these people resented Mike's professional and financial status, and that this could have contributed to their racial animosity—the idea being that racism is more prevalent among those with lower incomes and less education. But as we've noted, racism is just as pronounced among well-schooled professional people. I saw it in my first boss, Harry. It was there in my family's friend, the Mayor. It was obvious among the white educators at Bowdoin. I see it every day in the law, and a black lawyer sees it much more clearly than I do. The black lawyer has to face the white judge, and endure the indignities of white opposing counsel. A black trial lawyer must consider race in jury selection—his and the potential juror's. Again he must think of race and its effects whenever he examines a witness.

A white lawyer considers this too, but this is where prejudice differs from racism. The white lawyer practices within a white power structure. She has to consider African American attitudes about her and her client, but she knows that for the most part the legal system presumes the best of her client until proven otherwise. The black attorney is in the opposite position. If she can find a court that will give her and her client a relatively fair shake, she considers herself lucky.

Mike's experience at Cheshire wasn't unusual. In the courthouse Mike's been mistaken for a defendant more than once. He has to show his ID at every checkpoint, where I, a white lawyer, sail through. He's had to strip off his shoes, belt, and so on, in courts where he routinely practices. In some of these courts I'm a stranger, but as a white lawyer I get inside on nothing more than a nod and a smile. Even my white paralegals encounter less resistance than Mike gets. According to our justice system everyone is equal, but the people in that system have a hard time putting that into practice. In courts that Mike appears in regularly, the whites still fail to see him as in individual.

Racism plays a part in every profession. Any black doctor can tell you how nervous many white patients are when touched by black hands. Black teachers find that they have to find creative ways to gain the respect of white students. In sports we see this play out on a public stage. Everyone knows that Jackie Robinson broke baseball's color line, but it took almost three more decades before the sport got it's first black manager, and even longer before any Blacks reached the top positions in a Major League front office.

Blinded by the White

The highest echelons of corporations, courts, legislatures and nonprofits are far more white than the general population. Blacks still occupy little more than a token percentage of top management positions in education, science, and the arts. Even in most international forums whites rule.

One evening a few years ago my wife, Danielle, and I were watching the news. On came a report on the final communiqué from a summit meeting. In a post-meeting show of unity presidents and prime ministers from the world's most powerful nations crowded onto a stage. Danielle watched as the camera panned across the rows of pale white faces. As it reached the last ones, she said: "Look at how we're taking over the world."

+ + +

The "ideal" of color-blindness has skewed our thinking so completely that changing it requires work and self-discipline. In refusing to see color, we refuse to accept any links between race and inequality. For instance, if you, a white person, live in a town whose population is mostly white, that will affect who and what you see. When you go to a good restaurant most of the diners will be white. Almost all of the people who live on your block will be white, and, almost all of your children's classmates are white. If you live in a more integrated neighborhood, think of which parents you are friends with, socialize with and who your children befriend.

If you want to get a better, and more personal understanding of how race works in your world, start doing a simple exercise in reverse color-blindness: Every time you enter a room full of people, do a quick calculation of the proportion of whites-to-Blacks. Go further, and look at these proportions in terms of what people are doing. Who's working what job? Who's serving? Who's being served? Who can be seen? Who's behind the scenes? How does this stack up with the overall racial make-up of the community? For instance, in the town that's half-black/

half-white, if there are 20 diners in a restaurant, and 19 are white, that should seem odd. If there are 4 servers, and all are white, that should seem odd. If there are 10 people working in the kitchen, and 9 are black, that should seem very odd.

Odd, yet normal. As you do this exercise you will find the above proportions aren't remarkable at all. Whites tend to dine with whites. When their waitress is setting a plate in front of them, they prefer her face to be white. Much like my old boss, the restaurant owner prefers hiring white servers because they are the face of the business. He wants a white clientele, and he assumes that black servers might discourage whites from coming in. But he does hire Blacks. They make up over half the staff. They are the cooks, helpers, and dishwashers—help that's seldom seen out on the floor.

With each business the proportions change, but the principle stays the same: in a white business there are white jobs and then there are the jobs anyone can do. The white-owned drugstore in the white neighborhood will draw a clientele that's almost all white. You might also notice that the people working in the pharmacy are white. If a black works there it's likely that he or she drives the delivery van, or stocks shelves. An African American might work a cash register, but it's more likely to be the one at the candy counter than the one at the pharmacy.

This is where we are a half a century after the Civil Rights Movement. This is what all of that legislation produced. The law forbids hiring according to racial bias. It says that a public business must serve anyone, no matter what their race. The law requires equal access to public education, the ballot, and housing. None of these requirements has been met.

As the majority in numbers and in power, we still hold on to what we have. We do it by creating our own communities wherever we go. Some of our efforts are conscious, such as when we hire a white ticket-taker or hostess, or a black janitor or cook. At such moments most of us know what we're doing, and some of us might even admit that it's discriminatory. But our motivations for other actions are often unconscious. What were the proportions of black-to-white patrons in the last five restaurants you ate in, or hotels you slept in, or theatres, drugstores, or even hardware stores you frequented. In most cases you'll realize that you're a white among whites. You might protest that you didn't decide to make these places all-white, and you'll be right. That choice required teamwork. We did it together, and we continue to do it every day.

Chapter Seven

◆

Post-Racial America Through Black Eyes

In the years since America elected Barack Obama to the Presidency, some whites have taken that as the sign that our country has finally reached a post-racial state. I'll be the first to admit that I was pleasantly surprised by his election. I did not think I would see a black man or woman elected president in my lifetime.

Obama's election shows the great strides America has made over the past 400 years. It's important in symbol and substance. Millions of white people have placed their trust in him to run the country. Now that he has been elected and re-elected, any black child can dream of becoming president. Those of us who hear children speak of such dreams need not hesitate in acknowledging their validity.

But how has his election changed the daily life for black Americans? What have white Americans done to erase those last, deeply-embedded vestiges of our racism? If whites are going to move forward to a less racist society, we must examine racism in all of its forms, understand its nature, and use that knowledge in our efforts to eradicate all the remaining racism within us.

How do we go about analyzing what we see, read and hear in our search for hidden racism? One method I've described is reversing the race of the characters/players in any given situation. See how things play out if all the whites are black, and vice-versa. That will work for specific instances, but what happens on a broader scale? How should white Americans approach issues of racism day-by-day?

I See Color

My best suggestion will be a big leap for most white Americans, but it is simple and necessary if we're ever going to face the real problem. White Americans should change their most basic assumption about race. Instead of making futile attempts to reduce race to a non-issue (which so many of us try to do by pretending to be "color-blind"), instead we must assume race is a factor in nearly every instance. So, no matter what is said, taught or shown in any black-white transaction, inject race into your thought process, and follow that thread of logic wherever it goes.

What if we tried this for a week? What if, instead of automatically raising our old, stale defenses, we actually presume that most situations have a racial component? What if, instead of trotting out our usual reflexive, automated replies, we take the opposite tack, and assume that race plays a role here?

For example: MSNBC ran a series of promos where the hosts spoke in support of that network's "Lean Forward" philosophy. In one such ad, Ed Shultz talked about how our country is built upon fairness and justice for all. He said we need to return to those values. Think for a minute of how an African American would view that notion. Any black citizen would have every right to ask: "What country is he talking about?" Obviously not the one that African Americans experience. In another ad Lawrence O'Donnell spoke of how our country was built upon the immigrant experience of our ancestors, who came here searching for new opportunities and freedoms. This ignored the capture and enslavement of Africans whose subsequent "immigration" was enforced by legalized torture and murder, both on the deathly slave ships, and here in our country.

If we inject the issue of race into our most benign and universal statements, we can deconstruct the accuracy of what is said, and how we hear it. Look at the long list of white athletes accused of drug abuse—Mark McGuire, Roger Clemens, Lance

Armstrong, Bill Romanowski, to name just a few. Then look at Barry Bonds. It wasn't until he began his assault on the record books that he suddenly became white America's poster child for steroid abuse. When McGuire was breaking the home run record, there was hardly a whisper about his involvement with drugs.

Can we really say that the scorn heaped upon LeBron James for his change of teams is not race-related? We like to think it's the way he did it, but is that really true? James was a 24-year-old professional, who had handlers, agents, and promoters. Didn't those middlemen have something to do with it? We might express amusement at Bret Farve's endless journey from team to team in search of a title, but has he endured the same level of scorn as James? No. When we assume race is involved, these situations instantly come into focus. If black folks have a different take on Lebron, perhaps we should be asking: why? Is this similar to the divergent reactions to the OJ verdict? Once you begin to practice seeing things through a black person's eyes, you will recognize these differences automatically.

How often do you read or hear some sports person describing a black athlete as "a freak of nature," or as having "natural ability," "natural instincts," or "God-given talent?" When commentators make these assertions they seem to believe that white athletes are the only ones who achieve success through hard work, and intellectual ability. White athletes are perceived as exceeding their physical "limitations." Black athletes are perceived as simply being athletes. We constantly talk and write about black athletes in terms that demean their skills. We ignore their hard work, study and discipline, while celebrating the same qualities in whites.

On ESPN's The Sports Reporters a white writer commented that the New England Patriot Malcolm Butler's key interception in Super Bowl 49 was "an athletic play." The black panelists saw far more than athletic prowess, pointing out the hours that this man spent studying game films, his mental toughness, and his courage and smarts. Though whites might be blind to it, all of these factors went into this interception.

As you watch TV shows and movies, look at what roles, if any, Blacks are playing. How are they depicted? Are they criminals? Are they fully-developed characters engaged in real relationships that matter in the story? Or are they mere stereotypical window dressing, often comedic, and usually one-dimensional? You will see that black women are often depicted as fat, funny, non-threatening cardboard cutouts with very little sex appeal. Will we ever accept black heroes determining their own destiny, without a white savior? Or will whites always see black characters as needing our helping hand?

Think about what you've seen about Africa in the media. Do we still see most Africans as half-naked cannibals with painted faces? Does the white media ever show us a "civilized" Africa?

Many of us have some inkling that racism still exists, but to most of us this knowledge is remote and abstract. We tend to think of it as someone else's problem, but certainly not ours. Yet study after study shows the racial divide in housing, lending, education, arrests, police brutality, employment, health and more. We don't need any more studies. We see some of the truth, while ignoring far more, and the rest stays comfortably below our radar. We should recall that any depiction of African Americans as prostitutes, criminals, or fat, lazy targets of comedic barbs was consciously devised by a white director, producer or writer. These are conscious choices, not mistakes.

I live and work in New Haven where we've had scores of young children of color—many black, and mostly males—killed in gun-related violence every year. Yet, when we elect a mayor, we judge that person's success by the number of business start-ups, new construction, educational test scores and real estate taxes. If this carnage were going on in your white neighborhood or town, would it be acceptable? How many white kids would have to die before it got your attention? Or the attention of your elected officials?

Aren't these black children dying because we just don't care that much? Why can't we stem this violence? Whenever there's a natural disaster we make a special effort to rescue the displaced cats and dogs, yet when we drive by neighborhoods where children are being shot, we ignore the carnage!

Our greatest challenge is to understand how racism works, looks, and feels to our fellow black citizens. When the majority of whites see racial issues the way most Blacks see them, we will know we have nearly extinguished the stain of racism from our country and culture, but this won't happen until we make examination and reduction of our racism a daily habit.

Chapter Eight

♦

The American Dream

Something my father can point to with pride is New Haven's Santa Maria Maddalena Society. His grandfather, an Italian immigrant in the late 19th century, started the society to honor St. Mary Magdalene, and to bring together other Italians who had crossed the ocean for a better life in America. My great-grandfather's society has survived to this day. We go there often for dinner, and to be with fellow Atrani descendants from Italy.

When it began there were a lot of groups like it. During the great migrations from Europe in the 19th and early 20th centuries, newcomers landed in Boston, New York, Philadelphia, and other east coast ports, with no English, no money, no jobs and no solid prospects. Many had family or friends to take them in and help them get started, but others came with no connections whatsoever.

Of those who stayed in the cities, many wound up in tenements, or other slum housing. They took the worst jobs, worked 12-to-18-hour days, 7 days a week, and their meager wages were barely enough for survival. But they did survive.

They raised children who learned English as a first language. These children went to public schools, then got work much like their parents'. They might have suffered the same plight, but these kids were Americans through-and-through. They fought for better wages, and saved. Some started businesses, while others sent their kids to college. The next generation brought lawyers, doctors, and entrepreneurs. In just a few decades millions of families pulled themselves up out of poverty, and found the American Dream.

That history is pretty close to that of my own family, and millions of others like ours. We arrived here with next to nothing, and built a life. We had to fight individual and social prejudice, and a society where power and money were concentrated in the hands of those who'd preceded us: Anglo-Saxons and other northern Europeans. Despite these handicaps we made it.

So why can't black folks do it? We pulled ourselves up. Why can't they?

This question comes up in any thorough discussion of race in America. It's always there in the white mindset. If we can make it, why can't they? Why do they need so much help? Why can't they do what we did? We didn't need handouts. We didn't need affirmative action. We made it on our own. Right?

Our common heritage gives almost all white Americans a past we can look to with pride. That heritage inspires us to work hard, and strive for even greater success. With it comes our notion—often borne out by the facts—that each generation can, and should, do better than the last one. It was true in 1815, 1915, and it is still true today. That notion is at the core of the American Dream. Yet in the most material senses Blacks have lagged behind. Most Blacks have American roots that go back further than those of most whites. Yet as a group they still struggle mightily with violence and poverty. Two generations ago we opened our public schools to them, allowed them into all public facilities, insured their right to vote, and gave them every kind of help we could think up, and they still wallow near the bottom of our economy. What's wrong with them?

What's wrong is not in the people, it's in the question. It shows a basic ignorance of two strains of American history: our "white" history, and black history. It also shows the depth of our ignorance. We can't see their successes because we can't see the tides of history that they've had to overcome. This isn't just the history we learn in classrooms. It's families, and individuals, and their stories.

The American Dream

Most of us know that the first whites to settle in the thirteen colonies were English, with smatterings of other European nationalities. These were the ones who cleared the land, started the farms, built the towns, and rebelled against Mother England. Over a couple of centuries they built themselves a society. When my family came here we were up against that. Established white American families didn't much like us. They hired us to work in their factories, clean their homes, and cook, but they didn't let us into their schools, clubs or boardrooms. Just the same, we got there. Blacks didn't. Why not?

The role that our American history plays in the seemingly endless cycle Blacks find themselves in cannot be overstated. Though much of that history is beyond the scope of this book, there are numerous excellent books and films out there that cover it well. Those books should be required reading for whites, and we should make a point of seeing certain films. (See "Sources of Information" in the Appendix.) We must understand and acknowledge some basic history at the outset: first, we came here seeking freedom and opportunity, and, in many cases, fleeing persecution. Africans came to America in persecution and bondage. They were sold into slavery, and lost their freedom.

What does that mean? We came with friends, families, culture, language and religion, and had others like us waiting on these shores. Africans were separated from their families, beaten and tortured, forbidden to read, write, freely worship, or keep their names. Indeed, they were stripped of their identities. AND WE DID THAT!

By learning of the African Middle Passage, and the horrible conditions of their existence here through three centuries of slavery, we learn two fundamental things: first, that they have survived here and in some cases, thrived, is a miracle and testament to their strength and resiliency; second our own ancestors were cruel and brutal in our treatment (white people's treatment) of other human beings.

The questions multiplied in my mind: How does a people ever recover from the losses that Black folks suffered? What do they fall back on when their world collapses upon them? After we declared slavery illegal, did they simply become free, productive people with no self-imposed or societal obstacles in their way? What of us whites? How do our racial views and mental states advance so that we can go from treating Blacks as animals to knowing them as equal human beings? How do we progress? Can we free ourselves of generations of racist thinking simply by ignoring our past and "moving on?"

The fundamental question we must ask ourselves is this: why are Blacks today still struggling with poverty, education, violence, incarceration, and drug addiction? It's been over 150 years since the Emancipation. We are left with two possible answers: it's their own failure to succeed and overcome, which would imply that they are somehow inferior to whites; or, alternately, something else outside of them has, and continues to, prevent them from accomplishing what we have accomplished. We need to acknowledge our role in this second conclusion.

No, we are not enslaving black people anymore, but we need to question our treatment of them, our portrayals of them, and our feeling about them in an honest way. Are the only missing girls worth searching for white girls? Are the only high-school-age kids who get shot and killed white suburban kids? Will white traumas and losses be the only tragedies that interest us enough to become the fodder for TV movies and legislation? How do we change that? How do we move the equality "needle" forward?

A few decades ago if a white person felt strongly about the injustices of racism there seemed to be a straightforward solution: Take to the streets. The March on Washington in 1963 was the biggest, and remains the most famous, of the civil rights demonstrations, but there were thousands of others. Some, like the Selma March for voting rights, held the risk of violence, and even death. Other demonstrations were more sedate. But it was a time when basic, visible tasks still had to be done before there could be even an appearance of legal equality between the races. Would we remove the obstacles to African American access to the ballot box? Would a white Congress and white state legislatures ensure that black folks receive equal opportunities for jobs, housing, and public accommodations? Would recalcitrant states and counties integrate their schools?

The injustices were huge, broad-based, and clear, and many were codified into law. A lot of whites assumed that once the law changed, everything else would fall into place. (Almost all African Americans were more savvy. Black leaders ranging from Dr. King to Huey Newton made it clear that African Americans were probably much nearer the beginning than the end of this journey.)

Congress passed laws, courts handed down rulings, and administrators rewrote guidelines. Over time even the Congress, legislatures and courts became integrated, and recently many whites voted for our first African American President. Once these things happened, most whites assumed the job of rooting out racism was done. In truth, elections and laws are the easy tasks because they're so straightforward. We are now faced with the far more complicated job of looking into ourselves. What do we do about Dad using the "n" word? Or Mom talking down to "those people?" How do we deal with old friends who make racist jokes? Or Uncle Joe who won't even sit at the same table with someone who's black?

Malcolm X told whites that we should return to our own communities and educate our fellow whites about racism. His advice made sense, but he might have gone a step further and said: "Go home. Start dealing with the racism in your own home, and in your own family." Now it seems like whites are fatigued by the whole racism issue. Isn't it over and done with? Aren't we close enough to parity among the races? Do we as a people have it within us to take it to the next level? That level is a more sophisticated understanding of the covert racism in everyday life, a level where we, on our own, decipher and deconstruct the racism around us.

In our homes race leaves the public policy arena, and becomes personal. In my own life the issues have been incredibly close and constant for one simple reason: I dated black women, and eventually married Danielle. I come from a tight-knit family. I have a number of lifelong friends. Theirs is a white world. Yet my own world is one of a black wife, a black daughter, and many black friends. This difference makes for tensions that sometimes erupt into open conflicts. Sometimes we find solutions, while other times we don't. It's never easy.

I educated myself. I read book after book by black scholars; I attended symposiums and seminars on racism; I viewed movies, documentaries, television shows and plays whose central theme was race. And I exposed myself to these formats when they were simply about black folks and black life. I listened, and dwelled upon, my wife, daughter, and black friends' input and experiences on race. What that did for me was to balance the skewed picture that I grew up with, and what is presented to me daily in my life. I do this every day.

This has given me knowledge and perspective about race and racism in America. While I'm not completely free of my racism, or perfect in my analysis, I can often see it, and explain its impact, when other whites can't. Indeed, we often do that as a family. An example is the movie "The Adjustment Bureau" with Matt Damon. There's a part where God's "officers" explain to Damon that they came to Earth during the dark ages to move us into the Enlightenment. But then they had to return after we engaged in two world wars, the Jewish Holocaust, the Depression, Cuban missile crisis, and so on. In other words, starting around 1914, and going through the mid-1960s we had ruined the world.

When we got in the car to go home, Danielle, Alicia and I remarked that 400 years of enslaving and murdering Africans hadn't spurred God to send his officials to earth. Only the tragedy of white people dying was important enough to attract God's attention. It was only a moment in the film but it spoke volumes about our world view. Do other whites see that in the film? Only if we are constantly analyzing what's trumpeted as truth in racial terms.

Recently our local newspaper carried the story of a local Black man, Lubbie Harper, who had been nominated to the State Supreme Court. Justice Harper had pursued a successful career as a private attorney in his own law firm. He'd served as corporation counsel for the City of New Haven, then received an appointment to the Connecticut Bench in the 1990s. In the early 2000s he was elevated the Appellate Court.

When asked to comment on Harper's appointment to the Supreme Court, a local white liberal attorney opined that Harper had "street smarts" and that the Court needed someone like that. He added that the Justice always had a warm smile for everyone.

In the 21st century, a black man who is a doctor of law, with twenty years of private practice, and fifteen years on the bench, is appointed to a higher court, and his white ally sees his primary qualifications as "street smarts" and a "warm smile." It called to mind Malcolm X's quote about Blacks in a white world: "What do you call a black man with a PhD? N----r!"

It is precisely this kind of analysis that whites must root out of ourselves if we want to combat our racism. Only then can we offer instruction to our children, friends and family. The process of exposing, examining and rooting out this kind of thinking from my own mind was essential to me in raising my daughter. As I watched her deal with a racist educational environment I knew that, as a parent, I had to help her reaffirm her blackness and her heritage. In that role I owed her what any father owes a child: an environment reflecting the beauty of who she is and the accomplishments of black people.

What does that mean? Her art, books, music, movies, religion and friends reflect who she is and reaffirm her worth and beauty. Far from "reverse racism," this is what all parents are supposed to do for their kids – help them to grow up healthy and happy. Alicia is a beautiful young woman, inside and out. She's a college graduate heading for her master's degree. My wife deserves most of the credit for this, but I would've been nothing more than an obstacle if I had resented "racialization" in her upbringing. If I had based my parenting on a claim of "color-blindness" I would've been shoving her into the box where whites put all Blacks.

+ + +

Over the years I've learned that a person needs firmness, flexibility and patience. There are those times when you're forced to draw a line in the sand, but other times a combined approach of honesty and patience works best.

I've noted my dad's overt displeasure with me when I first began dating a black woman, and the fact that his attitude went through a change. This didn't happen overnight. When he forbade me to bring a black woman home for Thanksgiving dinner he couldn't even articulate the racism at the heart of this decision. He would only say that I shouldn't bring her "out of respect" for our family. It was only when I stood fast, and the conflict became a crisis, that he budged enough to avoid a long-lasting family fissure.

Over time it turned out that his budging wasn't a one-time thing. The change in him wasn't suddenly complete, or even from the heart. It wasn't that he was insincere. He wanted to do the right thing, but he probably saw "right" as making the effort to be patient until this whole dating-black-girls thing blew over. At the beginning I'm sure a part of him assumed that I would eventually stop dating black women, and that would be that, but over time his attitudes truly changed. I met Danielle, and my dad began to realize that our Thanksgiving dinner table was permanently multi-racial. The fact that he could accept this was a sign of better things to come. Indeed, he is one of the few people we trust with our family decisions. Often when we are faced with a difficult choice, Danielle will say: "Call your Dad— see what he thinks we should do." His advice is based not only on experience and knowledge, but on his deep and everlasting love for his granddaughter.

My dad has always been fascinated by history, and as Danielle and Alicia came into his life, he began reading more about the African role in the American chronicle. The gaps in his awareness of the black experience could surprise me (witness his failure to understand Danielle's mom's story of rest facilities on trains), but he was willing to learn. Now when he talks about the immigrants crossing the Atlantic he compares and contrasts it with the experience of Africans packed into slave ships. He understands that, difficult as steerage quarters were for our own ancestors, it was infinitely harder for the enslaved Africans who were crammed into the slave ships.

My mom spends many of her summer days down at the beach club where she is a member. On many days, Alicia will go down there and spend the entire day with her. Or they will go out for one of their lunch or dinner get-togethers. They have a beautiful bond of grandmother and granddaughter and have formed their own special relationship. Again, it wasn't that easy in the beginning. But I'm sure if you ask her, my mom would say she is blessed to have such a beautiful granddaughter in her life.

Not everyone has such a capacity for change. Dad's brother-in-law was an uncle I'd been close to while growing up, but that closeness didn't survive the racial divide. Racist slurs and comments had always been a part of this man's everyday conversation. For him those words and phrases were accurate expressions of his feelings. He didn't like black people. He wasn't always at our holiday dinners, but through the years we'd always known he might arrive at any moment. When he did we always had a seat at the table for him. Once Danielle and Alicia came into the picture, that was no longer necessary. He would still show up, often in the middle of dinner, but he didn't take the offer of a seat in the dining room. Instead he would go to the kitchen, where he would hold court for anyone who cared to go in there and speak to him. No one asked why he remained in the kitchen. We didn't have to.

Race became an insurmountable issue with my mother's brother too. He was the one who'd told mom he would've broken his son's legs if he'd ever brought home a black girl. Long after Danielle and I married, and had bought our own home, he still asked me to family functions at his house by sending my invitation to my parents. It was as if I were still their single son, living with them. That was his way of not recognizing Danielle and Alicia's existence. I cut off most contact, and stopped going seeing him. That made my parents unhappy, but they came to understand my position.

My siblings have a running joke about who's going to be stuck talking to me on holidays and vacations. They know that such conversations might turn to the sticky issues surrounding race. They've listened to my arguments through the years, and they will keep hearing them. I listen to their responses, and hope we'll all make progress. My sister, Karen, has shown a great curiosity about questions of race. Sometimes she and I take the long summer drive to Maine together, and I know that we'll spend the hours exploring her latest queries about whatever racial situations she's seen or heard about. Her desire to learn is sincere, and should be a model for others.

The American Dream

When a white American makes the honest examination of race into an everyday part of life, he or she will experience a variety of reactions. Some friendships will grow deeper, while others might sour. A close relative could suddenly become distant, while a cousin you'd barely noticed turns into an ally.

Or it might be more complicated. I've written about my grandfather and his gas station, and how my relationship with Danielle put him at a permanent distance. That wasn't as true of my grandmother. When I talked to them both about my choices, he left the room. She stayed, and tried to offer a tearful explanation. She wasn't about to openly oppose him, but she made it clear that this was his problem, not hers. While he was still alive she tried to keep her distance from our conflict, but she never shut the door on me. She recognized that Danielle, Alicia, and I were happy, and to her that was what mattered. After my grandfather died she told me that she knew he'd been wrong. After that we had many Sunday dinners with her, and a real love grew up between her, Danielle, and Alicia.

Every white American takes a different path on race. Some of us reach dead ends early, and stay there. Others make a U-turn, and find their way back to some kind of understanding. For one there might be a school crisis, for another religion plays a role. Sports are often the cause and cure of racial conflict. If you've read this far, you must be interested in solutions. I've given some of them in this book. There's no single way to solve the problem of race, but living a life dedicated to rooting out racism is a huge start.

If that kind of life is your goal, you'll find that several principles help when dealing with most race-related situations:

Self-examination: Don't expect to get over your own racism overnight. It is an everyday, lifelong process. Keep your mind open at all times. Always be on the lookout for lessons you have yet to learn. White people have spent several centuries building an incredibly intricate structure based on the notion that whites are superior. This structure is a part of the foundations of our white world, and might take several more centuries to dismantle. We are all infected by it, and each of us has to deal with it one detail at a time. When you discover pockets of racism within yourself, look for their causes, and root them out

Persistence: Because this process is never complete for white people, stay on it. Even if situations don't arise daily or weekly, keep reduction of racism within your family as a priority. Work it into your life like you might do with mental, physical, or religious practices. As you do with those, make it a priority and a habit. Thirst for knowledge!

Patience: Whenever we attempt to change deep-seated attitudes we can't expect it to happen overnight. If we're honest with ourselves we know our own internal shifts take time. If you see friends or relatives struggling with their feelings about race, encourage them, challenge them, and, as long as they are really trying, empathize with them.

Firmness: Patience is indispensible, but so is firmness. Don't be so concerned with understanding that you lose sight of the goal. Never compromise on the basic principles of integrity, equality and respect. If someone utters a racial slur or joke, don't be silent. You don't have to be long-winded in your objection. Simply speak your mind as clearly and concisely as possible. Be as courteous as possible without watering down the substance of what you have to say. If you can, tailor your comments to foster solutions. See how your listeners react. If you're dealing with people who have no intention of changing, then speak your mind and leave.

+ + +

Once we begin to make a habit of recognizing racism in ourselves and others, we can examine every aspect of our culture more critically in terms of race. That will help us discuss racial issues more intelligently with friends and family. That's when we begin to recognize racism in its most subtle forms. You'll notice how racism works in language, with "black" being a synonym for "bad," while white keeps a monopoly on positive meanings.

Always remember to listen. When you are with black people, pay attention to their concerns. Whenever they say something about race that goes against what you've always known, pay attention. Work to see it from their viewpoint. Put yourself in their position, and try to imagine how it would work if you were black, or, if they were white. Ask questions, and be prepared for surprising answers. Don't dismiss the unexpected. Examine it. Dig deeper. Ultimately the only thing you have to fear is the truth, and once you know the truth, then all you need worry about is whether you have the courage to face it.

Racism is a centuries-old problem that we can't expect to solve now, or even in the next generation. But perhaps it can be solved someday, and the most important contribution each of us can make to that is within our own lives. If we question our attitudes and actions, we can begin to change ourselves. If we speak up whenever we witness racism in others, we can draw their attention to the problem. If we work with our white friends to see the truth, and listen to our black friends with an open mind, we can change hearts, minds, and actions, bringing ourselves, and our society, a small step closer to racial healing. To me, that is a most worthy goal.

Appendices

APPENDIX I

SOAR STATEMENT OF BELIEFS

1. Racism and prejudice are not interchangeable terms.
2. Racism permeates all aspect of American society.
3. Believe that, as in any field of knowledge, understanding racism requires self examination, commitment and work.
4. Since racism is a problem of the white community, eliminating racism is a white responsibility.
5. Acknowledge that one key to understanding white racism is through studying the writings and experience of black authors and scholars.
6. Acknowledge white responsibility for slavery, and its effects upon Blacks as well as whites.
7. Support an accurate depiction of historical events, including the contributions of African civilizations.
8. Support reparations for African Americans.
9. Respect the rights of Blacks to develop independently of whites (i.e. separation).
10. Believe that Blacks have the right to define and celebrate their own culture (e.g. Afrocentricity).

APPENDIX II

20 RACE RELATIONS DISCUSSION QUESTIONS

1. What is racism?
2. Who is racist in America?
3. How does one become racist?
4. Do we consciously practice racism?
5. Why isn't being "color-blind" good enough?
6. How do whites control the dialogue about race relations?
7. Why isn't racism about economics or class?
8. What don't we understand about the black experience in America?
9. What are some examples of everyday racism in our lives?
10. What is the role of the media in perpetuating racism?
11. Why do more whites than Blacks think racism has diminished?
12. What are some of the theories of racism's origins?
13. How are we thought of by many Blacks?
14. Why are multi-cultural and diversity groups limited in their success?
15. How are black-only groups different from white groups?
16. What can white people do today to reduce racism?
17. What are some concrete solutions to improving race relations?
18. Can racism ever be eliminated entirely?
19. How many steps can you identify in the process of reducing racism.
20. What is your thought process in determining what's racist and what isn't?

APPENDIX III

COMMON MISSTATEMENTS BY WHITES

1. **Racism goes both ways.**
   If the issue is white racism, this is not responsive.
   Racism is the belief that one's race is superior to
   another's, coupled with the ability to oppress based
   upon that belief. By definition, only whites can be
   racist in America. Distinguish between racism and
   prejudice.

2. **I am colorblind. (I don't see color.)**
   Saying one is colorblind is part of the denial process.
   Everyone sees color. This statement denies people
   of color the respect and distinction of who they are.
   It makes their color "invisible." We don't say that
   about "not" seeing men or women.

3. **It's all about education or economics.**
   Racism affects Blacks of all economic and
   educational levels. Having a PhD or a six-figure
   salary does not prevent a black person from being
   harassed, profiled, followed or ignored. It does not
   prevent them from being discriminated against.

4. **My family came to this country with nothing and
   made it.**
   Whites came to this country looking for
   opportunities, many fleeing persecution and
   oppression. Blacks arrived in the chains of
   enslavement and have been persecuted ever since.
   Whites came to this country voluntarily, retaining
   their knowledge of their own culture, language,

religion and family. The Africans lost most of that
during the centuries of enslavement. Finally, color
was not a barrier for white advancement.

5. **Civil rights laws greatly reduced racism the past 50
years.**
Racism cannot be legislated away. The issue of white
racism has never been directly addressed by our
country. One need only look at the daily life of many
African-Americans in America today.

6. **I'm not responsible for slavery.**
We are responsible for the continuing mental,
physical, emotional and psychological racism which
keeps Blacks from attaining the securities that
whites enjoy—economic, social and political control
of our destiny. The statement also ignores the reality
of the lingering effects that slavery had upon Blacks
as well as whites.

7. **Africa is underdeveloped with no real history.**
Many of us are not aware of the fact that great
African empires were in existence before the Greek
and Roman empires. This is simply an issue of being
uneducated or mis-educated.

APPENDIX IV

GLOSSARY

A lot of the difficulty in discussing race is wrapped up in the language we use. Many seemingly innocent terms are code for how we see African Americans, both consciously and unconsciously. Their meanings are layered. These code words and phrases help us hide our personal feelings about race from others, and from ourselves.

ATHLETICALLY GIFTED: This phrase is most often used by sports announcers and reporters. It often goes hand-in-hand with terms like "instinctual", "natural" or "God-given" to describe a black athlete's ability. These terms minimize the work ethic, practiced skills, mental toughness and intelligence required of an athlete competing at that level. White athletes often are described as "intelligent," "gritty," "relentless," or "fundamentally sound." My favorite all-time description of a white wide receiver is "possession receiver"—as if all receivers shouldn't catch, or "receive" the ball!

COLOR-BLIND: Characterizing oneself as "color-blind" is pernicious in two ways: first, it is usually a lie. Of course we see black and white, and we notice it. While deflecting deep discussion, the term reveals a lack of honesty about the speaker. And, it also means that in order for us as whites to really see black folks, we need to strip them of part of their identity. We can't see them as who they are but rather some "sanitized" version of what we think they should be. The variant on this theme goes something like "I don't see you as black," or "You're not like other Blacks." Substitute the word "woman" for "black" and you'll understand.

INNER CITY: we use this as code or substitute for the

ghetto, which in most white minds refers to crime-ridden black neighborhoods. Yet neither "ghetto" or "inner city" contain color in their literal meanings, and often "inner city" is not geographically correct. Have you ever referred to anyone living in the "outer city?"

MINORITIES: See above, but this term is becoming increasingly inaccurate for world regions where whites are now the minority. Again, the term does not contain "color" in its definition.

NONWHITE (OR NON-WHITE): This term defines others by lumping them together as people "other than us."

THE RACE CARD: This is part of deflecting and diminishing any discussion where race comes into play. It implies that to inject "race" into a discussion is tantamount to playing a game, so we need not take the speaker seriously. When we become aware of how often race really does factor into daily life, this phrase should become meaningless. It also serves to demean the person (usually black) by discounting what he or she says, and it prevents the speaker from expressing or defining oppression of Blacks. Imagine using that phrase in response to women (gender card) or Jews (anti-Semitic card) each time they discuss a perceived bias.

REVERSE RACISM: If you believe racism still exists today, then there is no such thing as reverse racism. Leveling the opportunities for Blacks is a remedy not only for past wrongs, but for present day racism. The term also presumes that there is actually an unbiased, absolute standard for which we are judged and tested. There isn't. As an aside, where were all of these "reverse racism" experts when Police and Fire Departments were promoting only whites to fill vacant positions? How many white people do you know who protested the lack of black employees in civil service, private and public corporations or small businesses that remained all white?

SLAVES: Much like "ghetto" or "inner-city," this term has become synonymous with Blacks in early America, yet there is no color contained in its definition. More importantly, slavery is a condition, not the definition of who African people are or were. In fact, today we call cancer victims, Jewish Holocaust victims, and spousal abuse victims "survivors." We have come to realize and embrace the notion that their status is not defined by their experiences. So it should be with the enslaved Africans who were torn from their tribes, families and lands and have survived here. Remember, they were not supposed to even be here today!

UNDERDEVELOPED (THIRD WORLD) COUNTRIES: We also use "developing countries," though as "Open Veins" author, Eduardo Galeano, states these terms describe a permanent product of our economic colonialism rather than a specific stage. These descriptions assume that these societies are not functional, that they are backward in some way, and that the people are backward as well. These phrases also assume that we had no role in their "underdevelopment." They are arrogant, unnecessary phrases. (NOTE: We tend to lump together other peoples much like we do black people here in America. Be aware of how we use "Africa" to describe anything having to do with that continent, as opposed to saying "Kenya," "Ghana," "South Africa," etc. It would be like going to Italy or Germany, but only allowing ourselves to say we're going to "Europe.")

APPENDIX V

SOURCES OF INFORMATION

These are partial listings for two major mediums. There are many more.

Readers should also look for art and history exhibits, plays, concerts, readings, websites, and other resources that deal with the themes covered in this book.

BOOKS

History:

- *The African Origin of Civilization: Myth or Reality*, by Cheikh Anta Diop
- *The Destruction of Black Civilization*, by Chancellor Williams
- *They Came Before Columbus*, by Ivan Van Sertima
- *What They Never Told You in History Class*, by Indus Khamit-Kush
- *The Historical and Cultural Atlas of African Americans*, by Molefi Asante and Mark T. Mattson
- *American Holocaust: The Conquest of the New World*, by David E. Stannard
- *A World Lit Only by Fire*, by William Manchester
- *How Europe Underdeveloped Africa*, by Walter Rodney
- *Forced Into Glory*, by Lerone Bennett, Jr.
- *Roots*, by Alex Haley

Appendices

Autobiography/Biography:

- *The Autobiography of Malcolm X*, by Malcolm X, as told to Alex Haley
- *Martin & Malcolm & America: A Dream or a Nightmare*, by James H. Cone
- *Assata: An Autobiography*, by Assata Shakur

Psychology:

- *Chains and Images of Psychological Slavery*, by Na'Im Akbar
- *The Isis Papers: The Keys to the Colors*, by Frances Cress Welsing
- *Black on Black Violence*, by Amos Wilson
- *The Iceman Inheritance*, by Michael Bradley

Feminism:

- *When and Where I Enter*, by Paula J. Giddings
- *Ain't I a Woman: Black Women and Feminism*, by Bell Hooks

Social Studies:

- *The New Jim Crow*, by Michelle Alexander
- *Faces From the Bottom of the Well: The Permanence of Racism*, by Derrick Bell
- *From the Browder Files*, by Anthony T. Browder
- *Afrocentricity*, by Moelfi Kete Asante
- *Black Men, Obsolete, Single, Dangerous?* by Haki R. Madhubuti

- *Makes Me Wanna Holler,* by Nathan McCall
- *Enemies: The Clash of Races,* by Haki R. Madhubuti
- *Quitting America,* by Randall Robinson
- *Presumption of Guilt, The Arrest of Henry Louis Gates, Jr. and Race, Class and Crime in America,* by Charles J. Ogletree
- *Killing Rage: Ending Racism,* by Bell Hooks
- *Straight, No Chaser,* by Jill Nelson
- *Race Matters,* by Cornel West
- *The Debt: What America Owes to Blacks,* by Randall Robinson

Sports:

- *Red and Me,* by Bill Russell
- *40 Million Dollar Slaves,* by William C. Rhoden

Religion:

- *What Color was Jesus?* by William Mosley
- *What Color is Your God,* by Columbus Salley & Ronald Behm)

Appendices

MOVIES

- *Roots*
- *Malcolm X*
- *Do the Right Thing*
- *The Color Purple*
- *Daughters of the Dust*
- *Sankofa*
- *Glory*
- *A Soldier's Story*
- *Boyz n the Hood*
- *Rosewood*
- *Aqueelah and the Bee*
- *Drumline*
- *Pride*
- *Dear White People*
- *Imitation of Life*
- *4 Little Girls*
- *African-Americans: Many Rivers to Cross (series 1 – 6)* by Dr. Henry Gates

PBS FILMS/DOCUMENTARIES:

- *The Abolitionists*
- *Eyes on the Prize*
- *Murder of Emmett Till*

INDEX

◆

Index

legislation and court rulings, 69,
106–108
in public facilities, 91
racial
black-owned property devalued,
20
hiring and employment, 100–101,
105–108, 116
in housing, 52–54, 70–71
and Jim Crow, 92
in public facilities, 91–92
racism as the most widespread
form of, 69
residential, 69–71
retail environments, 94
why it happens, 108
Douglass, Frederick, 28

E

emancipation
legacy of
inequality continues, 128
as one-way street of racism, 77
plantation owners gave way
to landlords, foremen, civil
authorities, and teachers, 77
equality
accepted in theory, 45, 70
economic, 103
lip service to, 45
racial
accepted in theory but not in
practice, 45
in armed services, 83
blacks must deal with inequality
all day, every day, 82
Congress and legislatures
ensure equal opportunities:
jobs, housing, public
accommodations, 129
equal rights as gift, 83
failure to achieve due to continued
racism, 26
full freedom to vote, 129
laws intended to guarantee, 38, 44
nonexistent at nation's founding,
69
as readily available, 54
whites accept it in theory but
then move, or send kids to
different schools, in "nice"
neighborhoods, 45

remains elusive, 69
steps toward, 128
ethnic bigotry
and outsiders, 79–80

F

freedom
denial of, by whites, 102–103
"granted" by abolitionists, 83
owed by white people to black people,
102
promise redeemed in civil rights laws
of the 1960s, 92
religious, 69
sought by white immigrants, 29, 33
taken away from Blacks, 24, 29, 41

G

Gates, Henry Lewis, Jr., 108
Greenberg, Harry
law firm hiring, 99–104, 113

H

habits
changing behavior and habits
as most effective tool in reducing
our racism, 30
Hacker, Andrew, 27
Harper, Lubbie, 131
history, American
African American
has not been taught, 27
white ignorance of, 27, 28–29, 89
Black history
not taught in schools, 58
role of history can't be overstated,
127
sense of inferiority that continues
today, 20
white ignorance of, 27, 126
See also Jim Crow; segregation;
slavery
centered on white people, 27
difference between arrival of
European immigrants and arrival of
black slaves on slave ships, 23, 127
founding
discrimination in many forms, 69
post-emancipation
for Blacks
obstacles faced, 128

Index

Index

and failure of whites to
address it head-on, 34–35
having reservations is not
racism, 76
in housing , 52-53, 72–73
importance of admitting one's
own, 33–34
internal, 30
limit places where blacks
could live, work, go to
school, go to church, 75
mistaken names, 40
as most widespread form, 69
not listening, 93
opinions rather than
knowledge, 27
paternalism, 83
voting rights, 83
hidden
changing basic assumptions,
120
covert racism in everyday
life, 130
domestic workers as "family,"
77
hard for whites to address
because they don't see it,
22
learning as a way to fight, 30
need for whites to expose,
root out own racist
thinking, 131
racial divide, 134
steps to analyzing what we
see, read, and hear, 119
understanding that, and our
denial of it, as important
goal, 33
white blindness to, 22, 44
whites need to decipher and
deconstruct the racism
around us, 130
paternalism: "gift" of equal access to
public facilities; right to vote, and
open housing, 83
versus prejudice
Blacks can be prejudiced, but only
whites can be racist, 65
racism is not prejudice, 65
recognizing, 23
is always the color of white, 49

infects each person differently, but
there are attitudes common to
all, 66
language, gestures, and customs
of, 80
more oppressive than mere
prejudice, 73
more subtle forms, in white
assumptions
"black is bad; "white" is
positive, 137
one's own family as sources of
learning, 66
in race-based decisions
concerning
education, economics, class,
108
is white problem, 96–97
sources of
denial of, 33
white arrogance, 95
white ignorance, 25
by whites
and benign arrogance, 94–96
in everyday life
not seeing African Americans
as individuals, 41
four categories of, 26–27
as members of majority culture,
92
as a problem to be solved, 34
source of
as hatred or habit of
underrating, 110
racism, ending
acknowledging one's own as first step
behaviors, beliefs, and assumptions
hard to change, 129
as duty by whites, 20
essential tools in reducing racism:
desire to do so and open-
mindedness, 43
examining one's own racism, 46
first steps
learn about African American film,
books, authors, music, 31
learning to listen, 137
look at oneself through a black
person's eyes, 23
look at the world with an African
American perspective, 26

Index

understanding
  as process, 22
  reduce and eliminate, 23
racism, pervasiveness of, 43
racism, recognizing
  double standard
    in assessing athletes
      white discipline vs. black
        "gifts," 120–22
    in media images
      white savior vs. black
        criminal, 122
  greatest challenge
    how it works, looks, feels to fellow
      black citizens, 123
    once we make habit of this, we can
      examine our culture more critically
      in terms of race, 136
  as process, 22
  whites as "fatigued" by, 130
racism, solving
  learn to listen, 97
  must begin with ourselves, 97
racism, unconscious, by whites
  paternal elements are at the heart of,
    81
  paternalism may be the most
    prevalent form of, 83
  seeing African Americans as group,
    not individuals, 110
racism, understanding
  facing your denial as first and most
    essential step, 46
  five-step process, 47
racism, views of
  diversity
    as insufficient, patronizing,
      window-dressing, 19
racism unplugged, 49–63
racist thinking
  necessity of exposing, examining, and
    rooting out, 131–32
Rhodes, Cecil, 23
Robinson, Jackie, 28, 29, 114
role-switching, 97
"Roots," 41

S

segregation
  implicit, 70–72
    as ingrained and automatic, 72
  public accommodations, 91

public restrooms, 91–92
  on public transportation, 91–92
segregationists, 38
self-enforced
  creates many inequalities, 70
  through zoning, 70–71
slavery, 131
  abolition, paternalism of
    "granting" Blacks their freedom,
      83
  assimilation illegal, and sometimes
    punishable by death, 29
  events, conditions
    separation of families; beatings,
      torture; forbidden to read,
      write, worship, or keep their
      names, 127
  legacy of
    for black Americans
      means dealing with inequality
        on a daily basis, 82
  plantations
    core myth
      of benevolence and
        paternalism, 77
      necessity of viewing from
        slave's perspective, 23
      as paternalism, 77
      plantations, 23,
      denial of, 43
  events, conditions
    capture, confinement, and
      slave ships, 20, 120
    conditions of, 27
    cruelty and brutality of,
      127–28
    robbed blacks of their
      freedom and culture, 24
  history and legacy of, 14–15, 127
  Middle Passage, 127
    captured, beaten, and
      chained, 33
    white ignorance of, 28, 127
  post-emancipation legacy
    blacks not suddenly free, 128
  role of whites
    in enslaving, denigrating, and
      exploiting blacks, 34
  and slave families, 29, 33, 61
  white beliefs
    superiority, 23, 72
    whites contend blacks had no
      souls, 23